The Elements of an Effective Dissertation and Thesis

A Step-by-Step Guide to Getting It Right the First Time

Raymond L. Calabrese

Rowman & Littlefield Education
Lanham, Maryland • Toronto • Oxford
2006

Published in the United States of America
by Rowman & Littlefield Education
A Division of Rowman & Littlefield Publishers, Inc.
A wholly owned subsidary of The Rowman & Littlefield Publishing Group,
Inc.
4501 Forbes Boulevard, Suite 200, Lanham, Maryland 20706
www.rowmaneducation.com

PO Box 317
Oxford
OX2 9RU, UK

British Library Cataloguing in Publication Information Available

Library of Congress Cataloging-in-Publication Data

Calabrese, Raymond L., 1942–
   The elements of an effective dissertation and thesis : a step-by-step guide
to getting it right the first time / Raymond L. Calabrese.
      p. cm.
   Includes bibliographical references and index.
ISBN-13: 978-1-57886-350-1 (hardcover : alk. paper)
ISBN-10: 1-57886-350-3 (hardcover : alk. paper)
ISBN-13: 978-1-57886-351-8 (pbk. : alk. paper)
ISBN-10: 1-57886-351-1 (pbk. : alk. paper)
   1. Dissertations, Academic. 2. Report writing. 3. Research. I. Title.
LB2369.C275 2006
808'.02—dc22   2005031189

∞™ The paper used in this publication meets the minimum requirements
of American National Standard for Information Sciences—Permanence of
Paper for Printed Library Materials, ANSI/NISO Z39.48-1992.
Manufactured in the United States of America.

B H-C, you are the best!

Contents

Preface

How to Use This Book

The Elements of an Effective Dissertation and Thesis is for researchers who want to solve the puzzle of writing their doctoral dissertations or theses. Unlike other books that describe how to write a dissertation, this book separates the elements of the dissertation and provides you with a description, definition, and example of each dissertation element. It presents multiple viewpoints that include both quantitative and qualitative approaches. When using this book, you will understand *what* belongs in the dissertation and *where* it belongs.

The model for *The Elements of an Effective Dissertation and Thesis* is the traditional five-chapter dissertation and thesis. There are many variations of this model. Even in cases where the model is different, many of the components are similar. I have included many components commonly found in dissertations and theses. I present the components in a traditional five-chapter format for ease of use and not to indicate a preferred format for a dissertation. As a result, you will find a great deal of information you need to be successful in completing your dissertation.

In general, many doctoral dissertations or theses follow a similar five-chapter format:

1. an introduction, statement of the problem, and research questions
2. a review of the literature
3. the methodology used in the study
4. a presentation of results
5. discussion of the results

Within each chapter of the book, you will find elements for that chapter. The elements in chapter 1, for example, include an introduction, background of the study, problem statement, purpose of the study, significance of the study, overview of methodology, research questions, research hypotheses, objectives/outcomes, limitations, delimitations, assumptions, definition of key terms, and organization of the dissertation.

To facilitate the process of writing a dissertation or thesis, the table of contents and index are user-friendly; you can look for guidance with any particular phase of the dissertation by consulting the index. If you need to see an example of a research question, you can go to the table of contents, look under chapter 1, and find the section for research questions, or refer to the index. Since dissertations and theses share many of the same features, I use the term *dissertation* throughout the book for ease of reading.

This book contains samples from more than one hundred completed dissertations from well-known universities and colleges. Each of the scholars who wrote these dissertations has completed the journey. I have quoted from their dissertations not as exemplars, but as a guide, indicating how they completed a task that met the rigorous academic standards of their department and institution, leading to completion. These samples are contained in the highlighted Dissertation Examples sections of each chapter.

In reviewing an exhaustive array of dissertations, I have concluded that there is no one standard format that fits all. There is, however, general agreement to the elements that comprise excellent research. In the end, you must take personal responsibility for conducting your research and writing your dissertation. *The Elements of an Effective Dissertation and Thesis* allows you to concentrate on what makes sense and is important to completing your dissertation. Good luck.

Acknowledgments

My students' entry into the long journey to earn a doctoral degree inspired this work. I am grateful to them as well as to doctoral students, advisors, and committee members at numerous institutions whose work I reviewed. The students' success in earning their doctorate degrees and examples from their dissertations are at the core of this work.

In this digital age, I am in debt to those who initiated the Web-based Networked Digital Library of Theses and Dissertations (NDLTD). Because of their efforts, I was able to access and review dissertations from universities throughout the world.

I am grateful to my colleague, Dr. Sally J. Zepeda of the University of Georgia, who spent a significant amount of time commenting on this work and providing invaluable insights and advice regarding her experiences in guiding qualitative and mixed-methods dissertations.

I am also grateful to several colleagues who reviewed this work and provided me with important insights: Dr. Clement Seldin, University of Massachusetts–Amherst; Dr. Patti Chance, University of Nevada–Las Vegas; Dr. Max Heim, former dean of Mississippi State University; and Dr. Linda Catelli, Dowling College, Oakdale, New York.

I especially want to express my sincerest gratitude to Dr. Thomas F. Koerner, editorial director at Rowman & Littlefield Education. Tom has supported and encouraged me whenever I talked with him about a new idea. Others at Rowman & Littlefield have been supportive, among them Kellie Hagan, who was a source of encouragement and dedication to ensuring that the final product was of high quality.

I also want to thank Babe Hampton for her copyediting and myriad of suggestions for this work.

Dissertation Title

The dissertation title briefly informs the reader of the content and intent of the researcher's study. According to the American Psychological Association (2001), "The title is a concise statement of the main topic and should identify the actual variables or theoretical issues under investigation and the relationship between them" (pp. 10–11). It is important to use caution when choosing your title. A long rambling title, for example, may not convey the essence of your study. Remember, too, that the dissertation title's descriptors aid in indexing the dissertation to facilitate electronic access by other researchers interested in the study (Colorado State University, 2001; University of the Witwatersrand, 2005). The following questions are a guide to creating an effective title:

- Does the title present the focus of the study's research?
- Does the title give the reader a sense of anticipation that the study is important?

- Does the title indicate the study's methodology?
- Does the title contain only essential words?

Dissertation Examples

1. "The Effects of an Interdisciplinary Project on Student Learning of Natural Selection." (Durand, 2004)
2. "The Impact of Self-Esteem on Academic Achievement and Aspirations of Urban Minority Adolescents." (Partington, 2004)

Dissertation Abstract

The dissertation abstract is a brief description of the researcher's dissertation. It is accurate, self-contained, concise, and specific (American Psychological Association, 2001). The abstract requires you to condense your work to less than two pages. Many dissertation abstracts are no more than 350 words, so brevity is important. Conceptualizing and writing the abstract assists you in informing the reader about the study, methodology, results, and conclusions.

A well-written abstract effectively summarizes the study. Some contend that a well-written abstract contains five basic components: problem statement, rationale for the study, methodology, results, and conclusions (Koopman, 1997). In many dissertations where brevity is an issue, the abstract is comprised of just four sections: purpose of the study, methodology, results, and conclusions. The following schema takes the researcher through a systematic process in writing the abstract and concludes with a complete abstract with the four basic features mentioned above.

Begin the abstract by briefly restating the problem statement.

Dissertation Examples: Abstract—Study's Problem Statement

1. "This ethnographic in nature study explores how two middle school science teachers who have classes populated by urban African Americans teach their students and how their students perceive their teaching." (Bondima, 2004, para. 1)
2. "This study was conducted to investigate the possible relationship between exercise lifestyles and the overall experience of anxiety in a college setting." (Preiss, 2004, para. 1)
3. "This study examined emotion management skills in anxious children and their mothers and investigated factors within the child and the parent, and the child-parent relationship that may relate to the development of adaptive emotion management." (Suveg, 2003, para. 1)

Next, provide a brief rationale of why the study is important.

Dissertation Examples: Abstract—Study's Rationale

1. "In the dynamic, competitive environment of the leisure and recreation industry it is becoming increasingly im-

portant to understand employees' work motivation in order to increase employee effectiveness. Managers in leisure and recreation organizations must understand those elements that influence work motivation, especially as related to seasonal and part time employees. As this segment of the leisure and recreation industry continues to grow, it becomes increasingly important to overall organizational success. Yet, there has been little research done in any discipline pertaining to the motivation of seasonal and part time employees." (DeGraaf, 1992, para. 1)

2. "Throughout the nation, many political and industrial leaders are urging a technological transformation of America's educational system. Various current publications and articles have identified this transformation of our schools as necessary for continuation of our status as a world leader. A key element in the transformation of schools is the implementation of an intervention and the continued attention to the user's needs regarding the intervention's implementation." (McEachern, 1990, para. 1)

Identify the methodology and include variables, population, methods, and data analysis.

Dissertation Examples: Abstract—Study's Methodology

1. "The causal-comparative research method was used. A questionnaire was mailed to fifty-eight school systems in

Massachusetts, which were identified by the State Department of Education as having experienced a change in grade structure during 1981–82. A total of forty-three responded constituting a return rate of 74%. Part I of the questionnaire requested demographic, factual information regarding the school system. Part II requested information regarding the specific nature of the grade change and an opinion regarding the educational value of the change. The respondents in Part III were asked to identify the environmental factors they perceived to have influenced the decision. Analysis of variance was used to test the null hypotheses at a .01 level of significance." (Charlton, 1986, para. 2)

2. "There were 10 participants in the experimental (forgiveness education) group and 10 participants in the control (alternative education) group. Participants had all been divorced or permanently separated for at least two years from their former abusive spouse or partner. Ages ranged from 32 to 54 years, with a mean age of 44.95 (SD = 7.01). A matched, yoked, randomized, experimental-control group design was used. Participants were matched on age, duration of abusive relationship, time since permanent separation or divorce, current contact with the former abuser, and categories of psychological abuse. Each participant had weekly one-hour sessions (both forgiveness and alternative treatment) with the intervener based on a protocol specific to each treatment. The Enright For-

giveness Process Model was adapted to an intervention manual for this population as a protocol for the forgiveness intervention sessions." (Reed, 2004, para. 1)

In the next section of the abstract, identify the study's results.

Dissertation Example: Abstract—Study's Results

"Regression analysis revealed that AS predicted depression over time, and each specific factor of AS predicted depression across time. A longitudinal relation between AS and panic approached significance across time, and the Mental Incapacitation Concerns and Social Concerns factors of AS significantly predicted panic endorsement over time. Panic severity and anxiolytic alcohol expectancies were not predicted by AS. Finally, AS scores were stable across time points, though small fluctuations in scores were noted." (Carpiniello, 2004, para. 2)

Complete the abstract by identifying the conclusions.

Dissertation Examples: Abstract—Study's Conclusions

1. "In summary, the results confirm that migraine sufferers are more sensitive to intense visual stimulation than controls, but do not support the contention that exposure results in widespread autonomic changes. Since interictal visual

discomfort is a common in migraine, further research is needed to clarify how it can be incorporated into models of migraine pathophysiology." (Crotogino, 2002, para. 5)

2. "Analysis of the data suggests a strong, positive relationship among (1) the nature of the change (a re-branding that was viewed positively by participants), (2) the credibility of the leaders was evident in their communication throughout the change process, and (3) the change communication process was perceived as well structured by participants." (Gradwell, 2004, para. 3)

The following is an example of a complete abstract.

Dissertation Example: Complete Abstract

"The purpose of this study was to examine the supervision and evaluation of principals by superintendents in light of accountability and low performing schools. The researcher sought to understand both the policy and implementation of principal evaluation through a survey administered to gain knowledge of implementation of policy. Superintendents from school systems across the state of Georgia (N = 146) were surveyed about their supervisory and evaluative practices related to principals of low performing, Title I schools before and after the school received the low performing ('in needs of improvement') status. Additionally, data were collected for superintendents' supervisory and evaluative practices of principals of Title I performing schools so that comparisons could be made. The mixed method approach allowed for the collection and analysis of qualitative and quantitative data. Structured interviews of five superintendents were conducted to gain perspectives of the superintendents' practices of supervision and evaluation of principals of Title I schools. The qualitative data collected from the interviews were combined with the current related literature of principal evaluation and supervision for the formulation of a survey instrument called the Survey of Superintendent's Supervisory and Evaluative Practices of Principals. The responses from the statewide survey plus demographic data were analyzed using both descriptive and inferential statistics. The findings of the qualitative data collected from the interviews (N = 5) aided in understanding the quantitative data collected from the surveys (N = 105) which yielded statistically significant results finding that both the superintendents' supervisory and evaluative practices changed after a Title I school became low performing. Moreover, superintendents' supervisory and evaluative practices of principals of Title I schools that remained performing did not change to the same degree as did for the low performing schools. The findings of the study will assist superintendents as they respond to schools in need of improvement and accountability policy mandates. For policy makers, an understanding of the supervisory and evaluative practices of superintendents in light of accountability are better understood." (Mattingly, 2003, p. 2)

Chapter One

Introduction and Rationale

Chapter 1 introduces the dissertation topic and presents a rationale for why the topic is important. Some or all of the following components may be part of chapter 1; however, you should always consult with your academic department and advisor for the required contents for your discipline.

INTRODUCTION

The introduction describes the broader context and issues that surround the topic. It links the broader context, in a general sense, to the problem that you investigated. This is where you place the topic in perspective by providing data and a rationale documenting the need for the study (Walonick, 2005). The introduction may also contain the background of the study. In some cases, a researcher may choose to embed the background of the study into the introduction; in other cases, the background of the study is separate from and follows the introduction.

Dissertation Examples

1. "The 1903 meeting of a group of deans of women has been cited as the first organized activity of what was to become the profession of student affairs . . . and as an important milestone in the entry of women into the administration of higher education in the United States. . . . However, little has been written about the groups themselves. This study provides a description of the groups from the first general meeting in 1903 to the last conference's assignment as a subcommittee of the National Association of Deans of Women in 1922, using maturation variables of the Maturation Model for Professional Associations. . . . The resulting study builds upon past research to provide detail and clarify our knowledge of the early history of the profession of student affairs." (Gerda, 2004, p. 12)

2. "The aim of this study is to describe the direct or instrumental use of policy-relevant information in the policy-making process of the Chilean secondary education reform carried out between 1995 and 2000. This is a very peculiar setting because of the strong background in so-

cial research of the policymakers who were in charge of the design and implementation of the reform policy. The result of this study provides a better understanding of the type of relationship between information and policymaking that occurs when researchers who are involved extensively with planning and carrying out underlying research also play the role of policymakers who both identify relevant problems and devise appropriate solutions." (Tellez, 2004, p. 1)

BACKGROUND TO THE STUDY

The background to the study elaborates on the introduction and provides an overview of the study. Think of the background to the study as building the case for the problem statement, where you place the problem in an appropriate context. Cite antecedents and briefly describe the related research, while highlighting the key theoretical constructs you will describe in greater depth in chapter 2 (Baron, 2005).

PROBLEM STATEMENT

The problem statement contends that adequate information is not available to explain the problem or that a potential solution for the problem exists. It provides a rationale for examining prevailing ideas and knowledge with different theories or perspectives (World Health Organization, 2004). According to Clark, Guba, and Smith (1977), a problem "establishes the existence of two or more juxtaposed factors which, by their interaction, produce (1) an enigmatic or perplexing state, (2) yield an undesirable consequence, or (3) result in a conflict which renders the choice from among available alternatives moot" (p. 3).

Use the problem statement to describe the study's context, explain the rationale for asserting that there is a problem, and define the problem.

Dissertation Examples

1. "Teachers and students communicate non-verbally constantly. This researcher agrees with Miller (1988) who indicated that teachers' awareness of their non-verbal behaviors in the classroom help them become more proficient at receiving students' messages as well as more proficient at sending accurate messages. This researcher observed teachers' non-verbal behaviors used in ways that facilitated a classroom climate that helped at-risk African-American male students achieve. The problem of this study was to identify non-verbal behaviors used by effective teachers of at-risk African-American male middle school students. The focus of the problem

was to conduct observations of selected effective teachers' classroom interactions with at-risk male students." (Boyd, 2000, p. 3)

2. "Little empirical research exists that measures the effects of training on adult peer tutors, and none exists which investigates the effects of experience on adult peer tutors in post-secondary institutions. The question posed then is: Do tutors' responses to tutoring situations change as a result of training or experience?" (Sheets, 1994, p. 4)

3. "This researcher will examine the criteria that attracts and matters most to parents and caregivers of African American children with respect to selection and preference when making a school choice in one particular integrated, magnet school district of choice" (Anderson, 2003, p. 2).

PURPOSE OF THE STUDY

The purpose of the study offers a precise summation of the study's overall purpose. In some cases, this section may include several subcategories: research questions, hypotheses, limitations, delimitations, and definitions of key terms. The purpose of the study signifies your intent. Once you state the purpose, provide a rationale supporting the purpose of your study. This acts as a precursor to your research questions (Pajares, 1997).

Dissertation Examples

1. "The present study was designed for initial exploration regarding the relationship between various kinds of self-efficacy beliefs and purpose in life in a college student population. It was hypothesized that self-efficacy beliefs are significantly associated with purpose in life. Individuals reporting higher self-efficacy, especially beliefs relative to a college population (e.g., college, social, and general self-efficacy), would likely report greater purpose in life." (DeWitz, 2004, p. 10)

2. "The purpose of the current study was to conduct a comprehensive meta-analysis of the research on distance education in allied health science education. This meta-analysis investigated student achievement as well as student satisfaction resulting from distance education programs. Instructional design and delivery methods were investigated to determine components that contribute to the effectiveness of distance education." (Williams, 2004, p. 20)

SIGNIFICANCE OF THE STUDY

The significance of the study is your argument that the study makes a significant and original contribution to the profession, the scholarly literature, and your discipline. The significance of the study section answers questions related to why the topic is worth studying, how it may impact policy, and how it contributes to the general understanding of the theory in the researcher's field of inquiry (Ali-Dinar, n.d.). Further elaboration on the significance of the study occurs in chapter 2.

Dissertation Example

"This study promises to add to the literature on general education by analyzing the status of general education at the end of the 20th century, and comparing these findings to the previous studies, Toombs et al. (1989) and Gaff (1991). Just as the Toombs and Gaff studies drew comparisons of their findings to previous studies, the present study extends the study of general education on a national level and contributes to a chronicle that describes how general education is evolving. Finally, the present study presents alternative models for examining general education and understanding how general education practice and research might be improved. This chapter established the need and purpose for the present study, summarized its research questions, its design, its assumptions and limitations, and provided definitions of key terms. The next chapter reviews selected literature representing the extant knowledge regarding general education curriculum and curriculum change over the period studied." (D. K. Johnson, 2002, p. 16)

OVERVIEW OF METHODOLOGY

Use the overview of the methodology to present a summary and rationale of your research design (Glatthorn, 1998). The overview also describes, in abbreviated form, the methods you used to collect data. Identify the research questions or hypotheses you investigated, the research design, the subjects, and the method of assessment, observation, or evaluation; any instruments involved in the assessment, observation, or evaluation of the subjects; and the procedures for data analysis. In general, these sections are brief. You will provide a full explanation of these sections in later chapters.

Dissertation Example

"The basic design of this study was an experimental, pretest-posttest control group design. Participants were randomly assigned to one of two groups. Each group was given the same pretest measurements, intervention was given to one group, and then posttest measurements were taken on each group. The study was also a combined quantitative and qualitative design. The differing methods of data collection and analysis utilized in this study necessitated a combined study design." (Pariser, 1988, p. 9)

RESEARCH QUESTIONS

Research questions are common in qualitative studies as a basis for gathering rich and descriptive information (Merriam, 1997). A research question in a quantitative study seeks numerical data. A research question is distinctive, pertinent, understandable, and researchable (University of California, 2001). Yin (2003) maintains that the secret to excellent research questions are their substance and form. Substance is the description of what the study is about, and form is the type of question that you are asking.

Research questions are the basis for the appropriate research strategy employed in the study. They dictate the methods used in the study, creating a strong nexus between the questions asked and the methodology. "In qualitative research [the research question is an] interrogative sentence that asks a question about some process, issue, or phenomenon to be explored" (Johnson, 2003, para. 15).

Dissertation Examples

1. "How is university-community engagement defined by administrators, promotion and tenure committee members, and faculty members in the College of Education at Southeastern University?" (Baker, 2001, p. 11)

2. "What processes are used by administrators, promotion and tenure committee members and faculty members for evaluating university-community engagement scholarship in the College of Education at Southeastern University?" (Baker, 2001, p. 11)

RESEARCH HYPOTHESES

Quantitative research requires a research hypothesis as an integral part of the study. Hypotheses identify the questions that the researcher wants to test. Use the hypothesis to define and operationalize your study's variables. Moreover, use your hypotheses to create a link between your conceptual or theoretical framework and the research design (Clark et al., 1977).

The researcher typically uses a hypothesis to predict the outcome. The researcher sometimes refers to this hypothesis as the "alternative hypothesis." All other possible outcomes are referred to as the "null hypothesis" (Trochim, 2002a). Depending on the discipline, hypotheses may be stated differently (Georgia Institute of Technology, 2001).

Dissertation Examples

1. "H1: It is hypothesized that vertical ground reaction forces will be significantly different when landing in ath-

letic shoes with different midsole densities." (Nolan, 2004, p. 7)

2. "H2: It is hypothesized that loading rates will be significantly different when landing in athletic shoes with different midsole densities." (Nolan, 2004, p. 7)

3. "H0: There is no difference in precipitation levels between urban and adjacent rural areas." (Pidwirny, 2004, para. 2)

OBJECTIVES AND OUTCOMES

Some dissertations include objectives or outcomes. They are responses to the research questions and/or hypotheses. Generate research objectives and outcomes that align with your theoretical and conceptual frameworks. Objectives and outcomes establish a relationship between the study's central question and the research questions or hypotheses. Identify objectives and outcomes that contribute to previous research (Clark et al., 1977).

Dissertation Examples

1. "The specific objective of this dissertation is to study the control of the hydrodynamics and heat transfer in networks by means of theoretical, numerical and experimental methods." (Franco, 2003, p. 20)

2. "This study will produce the following outcomes: (1) a structural theoretical model and corresponding measurement model for predicting alumni/ae gift giving behavior; (2) a what if analysis capability such that if X changes in the model by Y%, giving will change by Z%; (3) a model that offers potential as a market segmentation tool for differentiating alumni/ae donors and prospective donors into definable segments." (Mosser, 1993, p. 8)

LIMITATIONS

"Design flaws are called limitations and they are what you should write about under the first subheading of this section. Briefly and humbly present the flaws in your own design" (Murillo, 2005, chap. 1, para. 6). Limitations identify potential weaknesses in the study's research design or methodology that restrict the study's scope (Colorado State University, 2001). Anticipate the limitations in your study's design and explain what you have done to minimize the effect of the limitations on the study (Karchmer, 1996).

Dissertation Examples

1. "This study is limited to data collected from records of the 1991–92, 1992–93, and 1993–94 school years. This study is also limited to public elementary and secondary

students. Under provisions of both the original P.L. 94-142 and the reauthorized act, IDEA, students under the age of five are included in the plan for educating disabled students. This study does not contain a cost analysis of preschool, early childhood intervention, and nonpublic special education costs." (Pringle, 1997, p. 6)

2. "The limitations of the present study involve participant sampling and lack of theoretical saturation; limited involvement of participants in theory development and revision; uneven degree of meaning unit analysis; idiosyncratic aspects of investigator bias; and the unique nature of bias toward social acceptability in therapists." (Baehr, 2004, pp. 327–328)

DELIMITATIONS

Delimitations are the self-imposed boundaries that you used to delimit the scope of your study (University of South Dakota, 2005). In this section, present a rationale as to why and how you chose to narrow your study.

Dissertation Example

"This study is delimited by the researcher in several ways. First, the decision to use a convenience sample of college students in the New York metropolitan area will limit the ability to generalize findings outside of this area. Second, this sample was selected from a public institution. Those students who are enrolled in private educational settings may bear different characteristics and, therefore, will not be represented by this sample population." (DeMarzo, 1998, p. 32)

ASSUMPTIONS

Most researchers make assumptions related to their study to guide their inquiry. According to Kennedy (2004), "In research, assumptions are equivalent to axioms in geometry—self-evident truths, the sine qua non of research" (characteristic 6, para. 1). In research, well-constructed assumptions add to the study's legitimacy. Some researchers, such as Yin (2003), refer to assumptions as "propositions."

Dissertation Examples

1. "Assumed is the idea that, if resistance to inclusive programs is to be avoided, attention needs to be directed towards identifying perceived needs of special and general classroom teachers working in inclusive settings. As such, special and general classroom educators are important informants about the availability of resources and support needed for implementing inclusive education." (Luseno, 2001, p. 3)

2. "Employees' perceptions of the training and development system are valid and valuable measures of how well a training and development system is functioning." (Kunder, 1998, p. 11)

DEFINITION OF KEY TERMS

"Key terms" refers to the specific terms central to your study and used throughout the dissertation. You must accurately define any such terms that may be vague or have a contextually related meaning (Georgia Institute of Technology, 2001). Typically, researchers include key terms that identify and explain the independent, dependent, and control variables (University of San Francisco, 2004). List the terms in alphabetical order, with citations where appropriate.

Dissertation Examples

1. "Collective efficacy refers to a group's beliefs and perceptions 'concerned with the performance capability of a social system as a whole (Bandura, 1997, p. 469).'" (Gage, 2003)
2. "Collective teacher efficacy is a construct measuring beliefs about the collective (not individual) capability of a faculty to influence student achievement; it refers to the perceptions of teachers that the efforts of the faculty of a school will have a positive effect on student achievement

(Goddard, Hoy, & Woolfolk-Hoy, 2000, p. 486)." (Gage, 2003)

3. "Middle School—A school unit that follows the elementary unit and precedes the high school unit; includes students from grades six, seven and eight of a graded school organization (Eichhorn, 1966, p. 107)." (Miller, 2004)

ORGANIZATION OF THE DISSERTATION

The organization of the dissertation begins by describing the dissertation's format and the content found in subsequent chapters of the dissertation.

Dissertation Examples

1. "Chapter 1 introduced the statement of the problem, purpose of the study, the importance of the study, limitations, and delimitations. Additionally, the conceptual basis of the study was established. The research questions were also clarified. Chapter 2 contains literature and research related to the broad topics that contain altruism and emotional intelligence. These topics are leadership and motivation. Methodology for this study is presented in Chapter 3 and includes the research design, selection of the sample, data collection tasks, and data analysis procedures. Results obtained from this method are avail-

able in Chapter 4. The final chapter, Chapter 5, is a discussion of the study." (Miller, 2003, p. 16)

2. "This dissertation is divided into seven chapters. This first chapter has introduced the general problem and issues under investigation, the approaches previously applied to these issues, and the unique approach proposed for this study. Chapter two reviews the literature that lays the important empirical and theoretical foundation for this dissertation. Chapter 3 develops the theoretical foundations for an ideologically-informed economic social contract approach to judgments of organizational fairness and alienation in the context of corporate downsizing and restructuring. A comprehensive theoretical model is proposed based upon interpretations of both philosophical and empirical literature, and an empirical model is introduced. Research hypotheses are developed that parallel this empirical model. Chapter 4 details a methodological approach to hypothesis testing. Samples, instruments, research sites, and analytical techniques are discussed. Chapter 5 presents the results of the efforts aimed at developing a scale designed to measure one's liberal or communitarian ideological orientation. Chapter 6 presents the results of the analysis proposed in Chapter 4. Post-hoc analysis is presented in this chapter. Chapter 7, the last chapter, discusses implications of this research and suggests further research possibilities." (Watson, 1997, pp. 15–16)

Chapter Two

Review of Literature

In many dissertations, a review of the literature occurs in chapter 2. There are several ways to organize a literature review. This chapter provides a clear understanding of how to go about conducting a literature review and a suggested organizational schema for the dissertation. In general, the literature review assimilates, summarizes, and synthesizes published scholarly research through the researcher's choice of theoretical perspectives (Cooper, 1988; Glatthorn, 1998). The researcher categorizes and comments on what recognized scholars and researchers have published on a topic. The literature review must be organized according to a logical defensible schema (Taylor, 2001).

Cooper (1988) suggests that a literature review reports published or primary scholarship. The scholarship may be empirical, theoretical, critical/analytic, or methodological. According to Afolabi (1992), the literature review includes landmark studies, contains a critical analysis of pertinent work, and has breadth and depth. The researcher makes a distinction between research completed and research needed, identifying critical variables, synthesizing findings, and noting important relationships between or among the variables. Moreover, the researcher confirms the problem context and significance, and places the study's research into a proper perspective. The literature review can be broken into three basic components: introduction, body, and conclusion (University of Wisconsin–Madison, 2004).

INTRODUCTION TO THE LITERATURE REVIEW

In the introduction to the literature review, begin by identifying your conceptual framework for the dissertation and establishing boundaries for the literature review. Provide the foundation for your research questions, methodology, and conceptual framework. In general, boundaries restrict the literature review to studies that are germane to your research topic, provide an overall organization of the review, and state the criteria used to evaluate the scholarly literature (University of Wisconsin–Madison, 2004). Often researchers find it useful to subdivide the literature review into major sections. Some researchers provide section summaries and then a chapter summary at the end. Many advisors insist that their students construct these sections, especially if the material is dense.

Dissertation Examples

1. "This chapter will begin with a review of the literature, which addresses variables that predict outcome in marital therapy. Next, the empirical studies on shame and perception of health in the family of origin will be reviewed. Finally, the socio demographic variables that predict divorce will be addressed. The purpose of this review is to provide an understanding of the previous research in this area, as well as providing a rationale for the choice of predictor variables in the present study." (Horak, 2002, p. 16)

2. "The guiding developmental theory for this work is that of Daniel Levinson. His work in this area was influenced by the work of Erik Erikson and his conception of ego stages across the life cycle (Levinson, 1986). Specifically, it was the view of 'the engagement of self with world' (Levinson, 1986, p. 3) across the life cycle that most caught Levinson's attention. Erikson's model of the adult life cycle consists of three stages beyond childhood: intimacy versus isolation, generativity versus stagnation, and integrity versus despair (Erikson, 1982). Each of these stages emphasizes a relationship of self with the world. When compared to Levinson's model, Erikson's intimacy versus isolation roughly compares to Levinson's era of early adulthood; generativity versus stagnation compares to era of middle adulthood; and integrity versus despair compares to era of late adulthood. Erikson does not assign

age delineation; Levinson does. This is one primary difference between the two theories." (Allgood, 2003, p. 17)

3. "This chapter presents a review of research and literature on students with Specific Learning Disabilities (SLD) and Alcohol, Tobacco, and Other Drug (ATOD) use, the development of social and resiliency skills by students with SLD, and demographics of students with SLD. Items selected for review address each of the characteristics identified for this exploratory study. The first review area includes a discussion of the definitions of special learning disabilities; facts and figures about learning disabilities in the United States; interpersonal, communication, and learning skills related to SLD; perceptions and problem-solving skills related to learning disabilities; alcohol-related issues with learning disabilities; mental health issues; and gender findings relating to learning disabilities. The second area includes discussion of skill development and prevention programming relating to learning disabilities." (Smith, 2004, p. 19)

BODY OF THE LITERATURE REVIEW

The body of the literature review assimilates and synthesizes the scholarly literature germane to the study's topic. Again, researchers often organize the literature review into subsections (D'Angelo, 2002). The organization may follow a variety of formats: theory, methodology, chronology, ideology, themes, findings, or populations studied. The body of the literature review may also explore any or all of the following: competing perspectives, conceptual framework, theoretical framework, synthesis of the research, and critical analysis.

Competing Perspectives

An important component of the body of the literature review is an acknowledgment of the different theoretical perspectives related to your study. Most theoretical perspectives can be divided into four subsections: individual, group, societal, and organizational (Yin, 2003).

Dissertation Example

"Some researchers argue that race plays the primary role in creating and maintaining current patterns of segregation between black and white households (Denton and Massey, 1988; Immergluck, 1998; Kain, 1987), while others contend that the racial gap in homeownership has more to do with groups' economic disparities than with the persistence of racial discrimination (Wilson, 1987). According to Wilson's arguments, the decreased ability of black compared to white families to purchase a home is reflected in segregated neighborhoods, because some residential areas require more money to move into them than others (i.e., more expensive homes). For those who believe forms of racial discrimination continue to shape where blacks and whites live in relation to each other, these average economic differences do little to explain persistent segregation levels in the US. Regardless of which factor one considers to be the primary reason behind residential segregation, all agree that current housing patterns exist within the larger context of history, societal prejudices, and government policies. 'Housing conditions are basically the result of the interrelation between resources of households, preferences of households, and the availability and accessibility of dwellings' (van Kempen & Ozuekren, 1998)." (Bond, 2004, p. 6)

Conceptual Framework

A conceptual framework has its genesis in the ideas, constructs, experiences, and facts surrounding the study (Krumme, 2002). Miles and Huberman (1994) define a conceptual framework as providing an explanation of the relationship among the factors, constructs, or key variables in the inquiry. Your use of a conceptual framework will allow you to identify a model of what you believe is happening (Salem, 2004).

Dissertation Example

"The conceptual framework developed here is based on an exploration of the relationship between people and the environment. We postulate that (1) the environment can be described in terms of its components (biophysical, structural, activities and general community elements); (2) human beings have a relationship with the environment that can be affective-sensory (attachment by identity, peacefulness, security, sociability, beauty) or functional-instrumental (removal or harvesting, pollution, development, access or distribution, nuisance, cultural relations, recreational functions); (3) human beings assess their environmental quality of life based on the satisfaction of these basic needs and personal requirements, attitude, experience and attachment to the space, cultural and historical relationships with the environment, the investment made to achieve the current level of quality of life, and the comparison they draw between their situation and that of other groups; and, finally, (4) relationships with the environment are associated with individual characteristics like age, gender, health, education, income, ethnic origin and marginality." (Andre, Bitondo, Berthelot, & Louillet, 2001, sec. 5, para. 1)

Theoretical Framework

The theoretical framework is comprised of long-standing theoretical traditions, theoretical principles, and the relationship between the principles and traditions (Krumme, 2000). In constructing the theoretical frameworks, examine multiple competing theories. Make a decision, generally based on your personal preference, selecting a primary theoretical perspective to support your line of inquiry. Once you make that decision, construct the theoretical frameworks, beginning with the theory's seminal works.

The theoretical frameworks connect to the problem statement and address the questions: (1) How does the theory provide an explanation for what you believe is happening? (2) What other theory(s) provide an alternative explanation? In essence, you are providing a theory to explain your approach to your line of inquiry.

Dissertation Examples

1. "I have identified three different strands of literature that relate to calling. The first is the literature that directly addresses calling or the experiences that accompany it. This strand includes several writers from different time periods whom I have arranged in a chronological sequence to get a feel for historical shifts in thinking about the phenomenon of calling. Secondly, I have chosen to review literature on motivational theory that I believe relates to the phenomenon of calling. Last, I have taken a look at writers who address adult education organizational issues that I believe relate to the way one perceives calling." (Collins, 2004, p. 16)

2. "Black feminism was chosen as the theoretical perspective for this study because it identifies the nuances of race and gender in the lives and experiences of African

American women. Black feminism, defined by Collins (1990) as 'the process of self-conscious struggle that empowers women and men to realize a humanistic vision of community,' suggests that 'African American women as a group experience a world different from that of those who are not Black and female and that these experiences stimulate a distinctive Black feminist consciousness' (Collins, 1990, p. 24)." (Beloney-Morrison, 2003, p. 29)

Synthesis of the Research

A synthesis of the research integrates what you learned from your review of the literature; here you indicate how the research supports or does not support existing theories and you raise questions brought about by your synthesis (Colorado State University, 2001). This is your effort to make sense of the research, where you identify patterns, themes, common findings, and gaps.

Critical Analysis

Critical analysis is your opportunity to evaluate the research and to provide your reaction to the research. Give a summary of the research, and in your discussion of the research, present your opinion of the strengths and weaknesses of the research to date. Demonstrate how you separated opinion from fact, examined a research design, and supported your claims related to the effectiveness of the research (LeJeune, 2001). In effect, you need to identify the gaps in the research and construct an argument about how your study will, you believe, close some of these gaps (Ormondroyd, Engle, & Cosgrave, 2004).

CONCLUSION OF THE LITERATURE REVIEW

The conclusion summarizes the literature review. Depending on the norms in your academic department, you may also introduce the forthcoming chapter on methodology.

Dissertation Examples

1. "This chapter reviewed the literature about how and why women are not equitably represented in educational administrative positions within our nation's secondary schools. In addition, this chapter attempted to illustrate that women tend to lead learning institutions in particular ways. Traditional bureaucratic organizational structures have focused on masculine characteristics. The call for more transformational styles of leadership which has dominated recent literature regarding successful school leadership has promoted the 'reinvention' of today's principal. Furthermore, research conducted in the last few decades has shed light on successful leadership approaches that draw from the research on women's styles of leading. Finally, the way prin-

cipals are evaluated has recently been reformed based on ISLLC Standards in ways that resonate with feministic aspects of leadership." (Thurman, 2004, p. 34)

2. "Regardless of what causes them, it is well documented that poverty and inequity in the U.S. exist, and that they affect people's quality of life. Also, the way in which both poverty and inequity are examined and measured, affects the evaluation of quality of life (UNDP, 1990). This study uses the Human Development Index (HDI) of the United Nations Development Program (UNDP) to measure the quality of life of single mothers on welfare in Georgia, and of the Georgia population as a whole by race and county. The next chapter explains in detail the HDI." (Alzate, 2002, pp. 47–48)

OTHER IMPORTANT TERMS AND ISSUES

The following sections provide insight into critical components—theory, scholarly publications, relevant research, criteria for selection of research, and organizing the literature review—that will assist you in writing this chapter.

Theory

According to Strauss and Corbin (1990), "Theory incorporates a set of well-developed concepts related through statements of relationship, which together constitute an integrated framework that can be used to explain or predict phenomena" (p. 15). One of the challenges researchers have in presenting theory to the dissertation reader is its presentation in a clear and succinct manner (Feldman, 2003). You need to be clear, precise, and succinct when you define the theoretical constructs relevant to your dissertation. If you decide to discuss, for example, theories of adult learning, you must clearly define your theory by supporting your case with appropriate seminal sources.

Scholarly Publications

Some researchers who are working on dissertations have difficulty distinguishing scholarly from nonscholarly works. A scholarly publication publishes original research by a researcher in the discipline, with appropriate references and citations, and addresses a research question or topic relevant to the publication's discipline (Engle, 2003). Since there is a disparity in scholarly publications, refereed journals are more credible than nonrefereed journals. Even so, keep a critical eye on the quality of published work.

Relevant Research

Relevant research has direct implications to the problem statement and research questions. If you were studying, for example, the effect of adult learning groups on levels of adult stress, you would examine research relevant to adult learning groups, adult stress, and the effects of adult learning groups on levels of adult stress. Follow the progression and evolution of research in your line of inquiry.

Dissertation Example

"The following literature review examines the relationship of professional development to teacher effectiveness in urban middle schools through the theoretical frameworks of organizational culture, organizational change (Schein, 2004), adult learning (Knowles, 1984), and professional development (Zepeda, 1999). We organized this literature review as follows: we framed the issue of teacher professional development in the theoretical constructs of organizational culture as it influences teacher competence in the classroom. As we examined the notion of organizational culture we looked at the theoretical constructs of organizational culture since it may impact the notion of teacher competence (Sarason, 1996). We then examined the process of change within the organizational culture. In this study, organizational culture and organizational change are reflective of organizations in general and educational organizations in particular. Within this framework, we examined the notion of adult learning, and then narrowed the focus to professional development for teachers in middle schools." (Calabrese, Sheppard, Hummel, Laramore, & Nance, 2005, p. 10)

Criteria for Selection of Research Included in a Literature Review

Another challenge for researchers working on the literature review is the dilemma of how to select research to be included in the literature review. There is an exponential increase in the availability of scholarly published works as well as other related materials available over the Internet. You may ask, "What literature do I review? How do I review it? What do I exclude?" It is important to simplify the process by establishing criteria for selection for inclusion at the onset of the literature review.

Below are two approaches you can take in establishing criteria for selection for inclusion in your literature review. Following either method will provide a clear set of criteria to use at the dissertation proposal or the dissertation defense.

Approach 1: Critical analysis of information sources. A critical analysis of information sources has two phases: (1) a preliminary appraisal and (2) a content analysis (Ormondroyd, 2003). Phase 1, the preliminary appraisal, is a filter that researchers use to include all relevant and scholarly information that meets the academic norms for their disciplines. In essence, your first strategy is to collect as much information from as many different sources as possible related to your study. Then assess the information you have collected against your criteria for inclusion. Once you makes the initial appraisal, filter the remaining research by examining the authors' credentials, the quality of the scholarly sources, and the depth of the authors' research (Neuendorf, 2001). Scholarly research that passes through this filter moves to the second phase.

Phase 2 is the content analysis, which examines the purpose and substance of each scholarly work. It examines the author's credentials for doing the study, the author's propositions for the study, the research questions, the depth of the literature review, the methodology, the legitimacy of the data analysis, and the results and conclusions the author makes based on the data analysis (Ormondroyd et al., 2004).

Based on the content analysis, sort the surviving scholarly works into predetermined categories. You may choose to base the categories on methodology, chronology, theme, researcher, organization, theory, or other relevant premises. Once you have separated the information into categories, then assimilate, summarize, and synthesize the information and draw appropriate conclusions.

Approach 2: Adapting the systematic review of the literature. Adapting the methods used in a systematic literature review is another way to establish criteria for inclusion. A systematic literature review answers research questions and has a defensible methodology for searching the literature, selecting studies, and evaluating the selected studies. Accordingly, the National Health and Medical Research Council (2000) summarizes:

> The purpose of a systematic literature review is to evaluate and interpret all available research evidence relevant to a

particular question. In this approach a concerted attempt is made to identify all relevant primary research, a standardized appraisal of study quality is made and the studies of acceptable quality are systematically (and sometimes quantitatively) synthesized. This differs from a traditional review in which previous work is described but not systematically identified, assessed for quality and synthesized. (p. 2)

Begin by restating the purpose of the study and making clear the juxtaposed positions. In the following hypothetical example, the researcher names the three variables in the study. By naming the variables, you are identifying the primary search terms for the literature review. Once you have identified the search terms, you will distinguish the databases that you will search (see below) and the criteria that you will use in searching those databases. Finally, you will then set the standard for inclusion in your literature review.

Dissertation Example: Systematic Literature Database Identification

The proposed literature search aims to identify, assimilate, summarize, and synthesize all studies that report on the association between _____, _____, and _____. The following databases were used: _____, _____, and _____. Only full articles reviewed by the researcher are included in the literature review. An extended database search will be conducted based on author, title, and keywords using criteria as listed. The criteria used for this literature review include: (1) empirical studies conducted since _____; (2) empirical studies involving the following populations: _____, _____, and _____; and (3) empirical studies published in highly respected peer reviewed journals.

Dissertation Example: Systematic Literature Review Protocols

"The Systematic Literature Review (SLR) applied protocols that involved a series of decisions as to which literature would be searched and which pieces of literature would be selected for review. The first protocol was the literature source. It was felt that 'pop' reports and opinion pieces were not appropriate to include in an SLR. An extensive search of the literature after consultation with the university research librarian suggested using electronic search mechanisms such as ERIC SilverPlatter, Wilson Select, ArticleFirst, ABI/IFORM, and Expanded Academic ASAP. Only literature driven by a research methodology would be included. Only literature having a salient bearing on the research question would be included." (Calabrese, Sherwood, Fast, & Womack, 2003, p. 10)

Organizing the Literature Research Search

The organization of data accumulated from the search of scholarly publications eliminates the chaos evident in stacks of papers, books, pamphlets, and bookmarked Internet sites. If you follow the guidelines mentioned above for searching scholarly work products, you will begin this organizational phase with a higher degree of clarity since you will have already made critical decisions on themes, categories, author, or other keywords.

Chapter Three

Methods

Chapter 3 commonly is the methods chapter. This chapter describes the research perspective, research design and its limitations, subjects, research variables, instruments and measures of data collection, data analysis, and validity, reliability and/or triangulation, as well as the methods used in the study (Karchmer & Johnson, 1996). The researcher should describe the methodology in sufficient detail so that others may replicate the study (Bradley, Flathouse, Gould, Hendricks, & Robinson, 1994).

INTRODUCTION

In general, the introduction provides an overview for chapter 3, indicating the chapter's organization and the researcher's intent in the chapter. In some dissertations, researchers restate in the introduction to chapter 3 the rationale for the study, explanation of the context, and research questions or hypotheses from chapter 1 to provide the reader with a macro view of the study (Walonick, 2005).

Dissertation Examples

1. "This chapter describes the research methodology, methods, and materials for this study. It provides a comparison of the two research sites selected and a rationale for their selection. The use of symbolic interaction to study leadership is included, as well as a description of the methods used to collect and analyze data. The application of backward mapping to this study is explained." (Gohn, 2004, p. 28)

2. "The purpose of this study was to compare and evaluate the preferences of individuals who viewed two different approaches to counseling. In one approach, a multisensory Rational Emotive Behavior Therapy (REBT) approach was used and in the other a traditional Rational Emotive Behavior Therapy approach was used. This experimentally designed study consisted of participants observing two videotaped counseling interviews. This chapter consists of descriptions of the participants, stimulus materials, procedures, instrumentation, hypotheses, and the research design used in this study." (Cain, 2003, p. 30)

3. "This chapter highlights the research methodology and procedures used in the study, which consists of the following

sections: purpose and objectives of the study, population and sample, instrument development and testing, methods and procedures, and data analysis." (Shao, 2004, p. 43)

RESEARCH PERSPECTIVE

You may choose to explain your research perspective in chapter 3 (Hakuta, 1990). For example, you may have taken a phenomenological, scientific, positivist, naturalistic, reductionism, or descriptive perspective view of your research. The research perspective limits the scope of your study and informs the reader of the boundaries that you chose to conduct your study (Yin, 2003).

Dissertation Examples

1. "This research study was guided by phenomenological inquiry approach. Since this study aimed at understanding the perceptions and experiences of teachers from their own point of view, phenomenology was an ideal guiding framework as it is committed to understanding phenomenon from the actors perspective. . . . In addition, phenomenological inquiry focuses on the question, 'what is the structure and essence of experience of this phenomenon for these people?' (Patton, 1990) and the study sought to understand the structure and experiences of the participants." (Wabuyele, 2003, p. 70)

2. "An alternative to the problem-based, deficit approach is appreciative inquiry research perspective that focuses on the aspirations of stakeholders where the stakeholders' aspirations are their dreams and ambitions. The positive nature of an appreciative inquiry approach was represented in this study through its influence on the methodology. The central premise of appreciative inquiry is a focus on the generative capacity of the organization under study to define and envision the stakeholders' aspirations based on the community's inherent assets (Cooperrider & Srivastva, 1987). Generative capacity is defined as the ability of the subjects, not outside experts, to identify and mobilize resources from within the community of study (Hall & Hammond, 1998). Cooperrider and Watkins (2000) cited the results on medical patients who focused on generating positive mental images and thoughts. These patients made a faster recovery. Cooperrider and Watkins assert that focusing on the generative capacity of the subjects under study allows the subjects to feel empowered and to shape their future." (Fast, 2005, pp. 14–15)

RESEARCH DESIGN

The research design provides the reader with the structure of the study, detailing the methods you selected to collect, record, and analyze data (Joppe, 2004). Here, you provide the reader with a detailed description of each of the research design's components so other researchers can replicate the study.

Dissertation Example

"The design selected for this investigation was a cross sectional design. Because the study proposed to investigate the effects of preservice teacher education on teachers beliefs and attitudes about teaching culturally and linguistically diverse learners, comparing groups was necessary to document the changes, if any, in beliefs and attitudes. Cross sectional designs involve collecting data at one point in time from groups different in age and/or experience (Krathwohl, 1997; Wiersma, 2000). These designs are not suitable for measuring change in an individual. However, differences between selected groups in a cross sectional study may represent changes that take place in a larger defined population (Wiersma, 2000). Notation of the study is:

N	EG1	O1	O2	O3	X
N	EG2	X	O1	O2	O3"

(Bodur, 2003, p. 22).

RESEARCH QUESTIONS AND HYPOTHESES

In this section, you restate your research questions or hypotheses formulated in chapter 1. Research questions often are addressed as how, what, or why questions. They are similar to hypotheses; however, a hypothesis is exact and indicates the measurement and analysis needed to address the hypothesis (Merriam, 1997; Yin, 2003).

Dissertation Examples: Hypotheses

1. "H01: There will be no statistically significant relationships between mid-level managers' perceived utility of community-based programming and NCCCS institutional location, size, and unit." (Adams, 2002, p. 34)
2. "H02: There will be no statistically significant relationships between mid-level managers' perceived practice of community-based programming and NCCCS institution allocation, size, and unit." (Adams, 2002, p. 34)
3. "Based on arguments presented throughout these three chapters, net deficits in both trade deficits and FDI in a given country should, all else being equal, reduce demand for labor. Therefore, I expect the relationships between my measures of net deficits in trade and investment on the one hand, and unemployment rates on the other, to be positive." (Ammon, 2002, p. 43)

Dissertation Examples: Research Questions

1. "How do preservice teachers learn from early field experiences?" (Olson, 2004, p. 5)

2. "How do preservice teacher begin the process of learning to teach as they move from university to schools?" (Olson, 2004, p. 5)
3. "How does the community college culture from the students' perspective contribute to retention during the first six weeks of attendance?" (Rasmussen, 2004, p. 6)
4. "How does the community college culture from the students' perspective contribute to non-retention during the first six weeks of attendance?" (Rasmussen, 2004, p. 6)

SUBJECTS, PARTICIPANTS, POPULATION, AND SAMPLE

In this section, you will describe your subjects, indicating their gender, age, race, ethnicity, and socioeconomic standing; use appropriate descriptors in sufficient detail to allow the reader to envision the subjects. You should also identify the process you used to select your subjects. If subjects dropped out of the study, provide the number of dropouts and their reasons for withdrawing from the study (Bradley et al., 1994).

Dissertation Examples

1. "African American and European American females were asked to volunteer for this study, only if they had already

chosen a college major. Students participated in order to partially fulfill their introductory psychology class requirements. Participation was considered voluntary, as other options to complete class requirements were available. Demographic information pertaining to the total sample of participants was recorded (Table 3.1). The total sample (N = 291) consisted of 133 African American females and 158 European American females. Ages ranged from 17 to 47 years old. Participants in the age range of 18 to 19 years, comprised 81.8% of the sample. Within the total sample, 239 (82.1 %) were Freshwomen, 28 (9.6 %) were Sophomores, 17 (5.8 %) were Juniors, 4 (1.4 %) were Seniors, and 3 (1.0 %) were in a continuing education program." (Bath, 2002, p. 53)

2. "Sampling method. Because the clinics and the hospitals are administrated by the same organization, communication therein is very efficient. With the birth of a child, the hospital sends a document to the health clinic where the child lives, informing them of the child's birth and reporting a brief medical history. If the mother and child have not appeared at the clinic within the first 2 weeks for a well baby exam, a member of the medical team goes to the family's residence to check on the mother and child. It was through these documents sent to the clinics that participants were identified for inclusion in the study. When the clinic received the birth notification, they informed the researchers and provided them with

contact information. All children born between March of 1999 and May of 2000 were considered for eligibility in the study. When the infants completed four months of age, a medical student visited the family's household in order to get permission to carry out a family interview, obtain demographic data, and check the inclusion criteria." (Hollist, 2002, p. 22)

3. "Participants were recruited who were nursing staff working on any of the five patient care units with the highest numbers of back injuries (two SCIUs and three NHCUs) and six patient care units with lower numbers of back injuries. This included all of the overnight stay units at the JAHVAMC except for the Surgical Intensive Care Unit, Coronary Care Unit, and the Rehabilitation Unit. The latter units were omitted due to reaching the participant recruitment goals from the units listed. The five high-risk units were 1BSW (SCIU), 5W (SCIU), NHCU-A, NHCU-C, and NHCU-D. The five low-risk units included four Medical-Surgical Units (4S, 5S, 6S, 7N) and one ICU (Medical Intensive Care Unit [MICU]). Additionally, ten participants from 2BSW, a psychiatric in-patient unit with virtually no routine patient handling and movement required, were recruited. (Some physical exertion is required on an infrequent basis during emergency restraint procedures.) This unit was included to ensure the inclusion of some study participants with limited handling and movement exposure." (Menzel, 2001, p. 27)

UNIT OF ANALYSIS

The unit of analysis is the focus of the study. The study may include multiple units of analysis (Trochim, 2002b). The unit of analysis is related to the study's research questions and sets boundaries for the study (Patton, 1990; Yin, 2003). The unit of analysis and its sample size are determined by the research design (Dallal, 2004).

Dissertation Examples

1. "An important step in research design is to determine the unit of analysis—or the unit about which statements are being made. In this study proposed theory, data collection and statistical analyses were conducted at the organizational level. Therefore, the unit of analysis for this study was the individual agency." (Akbulut, 2003, p. 48)

2. "The sixth goal was to test the presumption that cohesion and discrepancy reduction mechanisms interact to increase the congruence between the value system and part-time work experiences, or in other words, increase consistency within the person-in-context unit of analysis forwarded within the developmental-contextual meta model of human development. Finally, the seventh goal was to examine whether the cohesion and discrepancy reduction mechanisms promoting harmony between work values and experience varied as a function of person- and context-level variability." (Porfeli, 2004, pp. 251–252)

RESEARCH VARIABLES

In this section, describe the research variables you intend to use in your study, as well as the attributes associated with each of the variables. "Attributes are characteristics or qualities that describe an object. . . . Anything you might say to describe yourself or someone else involves an attribute" (Babbie, 2001, p. 17). Describe your independent, dependent, and any confounding variables that may be part of the study (Heffner, 2004a).

Dissertation Examples

1. "Based on the research questions and hypothesis identified for this study, several dependent, independent, and control variables have been identified. Further details of the dependent, independent, and control variables are discussed in the following sections of this document. . . . The dependent variables in this study were the perceptions of student-to-student interaction, teacher-to-student interactions, and student satisfaction. Both of the variables, student-to-student and student-to-teacher interaction, were measured independently by summing the responses to each of the questions identified on the perception of interaction. . . . The primary independent variables investigated were learning strategies, student-to-student interaction, and student-to-teacher interaction." (Bailey, 2002, pp. 44–45)

2. "The dependent variable in this study was the stakeholders' perceived level of satisfaction with the economic
   development strategies employed by the community colleges in their service area. The independent variables
   used in this study were categorized into two groups: the
   personal factors of the respondents and the institutional
   factors of the community colleges within the geographic
   region of the study." (Gossett, 2002, p. 87)

RESEARCH INSTRUMENT

This section provides the reader with a complete description
of the research instrument that you used to collect data. Describe each instrument, with appropriate cited references
supporting your instruments as well as their validity and reliability. Include references to other substantive research in
appropriately related fields where the researchers used the
instruments to collect similar data.

Dissertation Examples

1. "A demographic questionnaire was devised that includes
   questions regarding general demographic information, i.e.,
   age, gender, marital status, grade, major, ethnicity. This instrument is found in Appendix C." (Nicolas, 2002, p. 36)
2. "*Beck Depression Inventory (BDI).* The BDI (Beck,
   1978) is a self-report measure designed to assess for

severity of depression, with an emphasis on its cognitive, affective and behavioral symptoms. Presence of somatic symptoms is not emphasized, with only one such symptom measured (fatigue). The BDI employs a 4 point Likert-type scale (0–3) wherein 0 = absence of symptoms, 1 = mild symptom, 2 = moderate, and 3 = severe or debilitating symptom. For the present study, the total BDI score was utilized, with a range of 0 to 63 total score (a score of 15 or higher indicating clinically elevated level of depressive symptoms)." (Gaines, 2001, p. 25)

3. "Multiple items were proposed to measure each latent construct in this study (see Figure 3). It is customary for squares in models to represent observed variables and circles to represent latent variables. Each construct is described below following the demographic questionnaire." (House, 2004, p. 57)

4. "This study had two phases: a) identifying instructional elements existing in the sample, and b) rating courses using these elements. Identifying course elements involved a literature review spanning traditional and distance education. Notable design elements were recorded in a 'descriptors list' that serves as the theoretical basis for an instrument (necessary to complete the second research phase). This list led to a pilot study involving nine courses from five online high schools. School selection was based on school reputation, age, size, offerings, student types, and willingness to participate. Course selection included biased randomization, ensuring inclusion of all schools and subjects.

Because courses were the unit of analysis, human subjects protocols were unnecessary." (Keeler, 2003, p. 1)

PILOT STUDY

The term *pilot study* may refer to a small-scale version, or trial run, to test or assess a research instrument as a precursor to a more general study. A pilot study may work as a fail-safe measure to alert you to critical points where your study might be compromised (van Teijlingen & Hundley, 2001). Moreover, a pilot study can aid in modifying your data collection plans regarding content and procedures (Yin, 2003). If a pilot group has been used to test the instrument, describe the demographic makeup of the pilot group and the conditions under which the group piloted the instrument (International University of Professional Studies, 2004).

Dissertation Example

"The questionnaire design was piloted before its distribution. Copies of two proposed questionnaires were sent to 10 current or former superintendents who were selected because of their knowledge and expertise regarding district finance. They were asked to review the proposed document for clarity of instructions, preference for design, face validity, and other constructive suggestions to improve the survey design.

The suggestions gathered from this process were considered in the final design decisions." (Neill, 2003, p. 29)

DATA COLLECTION PROCEDURES

In this section, you will present your plan for collecting data. Indicate the type of data that is needed to answer the research questions or hypotheses and identify the use of equipment or other types of supplies. Also, identify tests, surveys, data-gathering sites, record-keeping procedures, and how you have organized your data-gathering methods (Ginorio, n.d.). In general, this section comprises four parts: design, participants, instruments, and procedures (Wong, 2002).

Dissertation Examples

1. "The data were collected with a survey developed for this study and distributed to mental health practitioners in a 12-county region of Southeast Ohio. The survey responses are presented, including descriptive data incorporating both demographic information and the exploration of issues discussed in the retention literature. Three-hundred-and-twenty surveys were sent out: 60 to one mental health center, 30 to another (together they covered six rural counties), and 230 that were randomly chosen from a list of individuals described in Chapter III. Out of the 60 surveys

sent to the first mental health agency surveys, 45 (75%) were returned. The second agency returned 24 of 30 (80%). Of the 230 mailed surveys, 98 (43%) were returned. Twenty-two surveys were returned because the individuals moved. Overall, 163 (51%) usable surveys were returned." (Meyer, 2003, p. 88)

2. "Attendance information for the current study was obtained through a retrospective review of the participants' medical records. Baseline data collection occurred between 1992 and 1995. Volunteers were consecutively recruited during their initial appointments with the HIV outpatient clinic. Participants included individuals who had been diagnosed with HIV and were receiving outpatient medical treatment at the above-mentioned clinic (EKL). Informed consent was obtained prior to participation in the study (see Appendix D). Demographic information was obtained from patient interviews conducted during the initial clinic appointment and from the baseline demographics questionnaire completed by patients. Information concerning disease status and other medical information was obtained through a review of the patients' medical records at baseline. Participants were paid five dollars for completion of the baseline questionnaires. Following baseline data collection all scheduled clinic appointments, including physician and nurse visits, were monitored via chart reviews for a period of three years from the patient's entry into the study. Appointment attendance information (frequency of

scheduled, canceled, and 'no show' appointments) was obtained from a retrospective review of the patients' medical records. When available, other important information such as changes in attending physician and reason for discharge from the clinic (e.g. deceased, relocating) was also recorded during examination of the patients' medical records." (D. M. Johnson, 2002, pp. 21–22)

DATA COLLECTION AND STATISTICAL ANALYSIS

In this section, describe how you collected, reported, and analyzed the data. Identify the data and then describe how you proceeded with your analysis. List your methods, software, statistical procedures, or qualitative content analysis methods (Ragin, Nagel, & White, 2004). According to Trochim (2002b), data analysis has three components: data preparation, a description of the population and the measures, and a description of how the researcher plans to analyze the data. Here, too, you will cite your use of statistical software programs such as SPSS, NUD*IST, or other programs and present a rationale for their use.

Dissertation Examples

1. "I used a constant comparative method of data analysis. As I indicated earlier, I audio-tape recorded interviews with

participants and had the interviews transcribed verbatim. Analysis of data began with the transcriptions. I made analytic memos as the transcription proceeded. I read the transcriptions and coded them immediately after each transcription. As I coded the data, I looked for relationships and patterns and attempted to fit them into categories. After I collected and transcribed all data, I reread the transcriptions comparing the responses of all of the participants that I interviewed. I searched for similarities and differences in key words or phrases, time, relationships, feelings and perceptions. I analyzed concepts for how and why the participants perceive school now, as well as how and why they performed as they did while they were students. I recoded and recategorized as new concepts emerged. As themes emerged, I began to interpret the data and developed theories. I stored data on note cards in file boxes by themes. I made copies of transcriptions to preserve the original, and conducted coding and recoding, cutting and pasting on copies. I stored and labeled tapes by dates and participant code names." (Carper, 2002, p. 45)

2. "An analysis of documents and existing scholarship provided information about international and national level notions and practices with regard to community schools in Mali (See Appendix A). These documents (including agency and donor reports, monitoring and evaluation materials, specific program documents on community schools from SC/USA, Ministry of Education documents)

revealed factors that helped shape perceptions of community schools at international and national levels in particular. At the international level, existing scholarship that addressed community schools or similar education strategies outside of the formal system was identified for a literature review." (Capacci-Carneal, 2004, p. 30)

3. "For the handgrip task a repeated measures (RM) multivariate analysis of variance (MANOVA) was employed with gender as a between subjects factor, and time intervals (15 sec) nested within three sensation variables nested within three clusters (i.e., physical, motivational and affective sensations) as repeated factors and gender as a between subjects factor. For the cycle task a RM MANOVA was employed with time intervals (30 sec) nested within three sensation variables as repeated factors and gender as a between subjects factor. A hierarchical linear regression analysis was conducted to determine how much of the variance in 'time to fatigue' was accounted for by dispositional and task-specific factors. The significance level used in this study was $p \leq 0.05$." (Hutchinson, 2004, p. 29)

SETTING AND ENVIRONMENT

In many dissertations, the researcher provides a rich and detailed description of the setting and environment in which the study was conducted (Patton, 1990). In describing the setting, explain how and why you chose the site. Describe the surrounding environment, if applicable, appropriate members within the environment, and any other circumstances within the environment that affect the study (University of South Dakota, 2005).

Dissertation Examples

1. "The first half of my study occurred in an urban elementary school, Frost Elementary, situated in the southeastern part of the United States. This school was chosen mainly for its diverse student population. Other factors considered were the constructivist philosophy espoused by staff, the organizational structure that allows students to change classes for certain subjects, and its small number of students. Approximately 500 students attend the school from 9:00 am until 3:30 pm. It is designated a gifted and talented magnet elementary school. The designation of magnet school means Frost Elementary draws students from the western and southern parts of the county to complement the students who are assigned from abase area around the inner-city school. Magnet students travel up to one hour each way on a school bus or by car to get to the school." (Godfrey, 2003, p. 81)

2. "My research was conducted in an eighth grade physical science classroom called the Computers as Learning Partner (CLP) located at Foothill Middle School in Wal-

nut Creek, California. While the school is located in an affluent, upper-middle-class suburb, many students who attend this school are recent immigrants from Russia and the Far East. . . . The classroom houses 16 Macintosh LC II computers only recently wired to the Internet. At the time of my data collection, the classroom had a local area network installed and a single modem connecting to the teacher's computer and telephone line. The MFK software ran on a stand-alone pair of Macintosh IIci machines housed inside a custom-designed case at the side of the classroom (Figure 5.1 and 5.2). One computer faced the front of the classroom and the other faced the back." (Hsiao-Rai Hsi, 1997, para. 2)

BIAS AND ERROR

In this section, acknowledge the potential bias and error that may have occurred in your study. Indicate the sources of bias, conditions, or circumstances that might have affected the study's validity. Reporting the bias or error, or the potential for the existence for bias and error, allows you to make legitimate conclusions regarding the units of analysis (Helberg, 1996).

Dissertation Example

"One of the advantages of a participant-observer approach is that the researcher enters into the world of her/his informants and is able to describe the complex system of social interactions. This provided the researcher with more of an insider's view of the situation being studied, helping to validate his/her findings. This same advantage can be construed as a situation that might encourage bias in the researchers reporting of data and so must be balanced with controls. Use of collaborative teacher-researcher provides an insider who can challenge the interpretations of the researcher. A constant check for rival hypotheses or negative instances also provides control. The use of value free note taking with separate personal and analytical notes provides a more unbiased approach." (Mather, 2004, p. 79)

VALIDITY

In this section, report how your study meets the rigorous standards of validity. "Validity refers to the accuracy or truthfulness of a measurement" (Walonick, 2005, chap. 3, Validity and Reliability section, para. 2). Regardless of your research methodology, you must address the various types of validity. According to Trochim (2001), there are four types of validity: conclusion validity, internal validity, construct validity, and external validity. Qualitative researchers, for example, may describe triangulation, member checking, repeated observations, peer scrutiny of the data, and collaboration within the research as a way of showing the study's validity (Merriam, 1997). An example of how one researcher described content validity is shown below.

Dissertation Example

"Content validity is the degree to which the sample of test items represents the content that the test is designed to measure (Borg & Gall, 1989 p. 258). In the development of the SEBEST, the items need to be representative with regard to the two dimensions of the self-efficacy construct i.e. personal self-efficacy and outcome expectancy and dimensions of diversity. As discussed earlier in Chapter 2, a diverse learner to science education is a person who has been identified by science education research (NSES, 1996; NSTA Pathways, 1997 & SAA, 1989) as one who has not achieved the success in science education as compared to their peers for reasons that may be attributed to but are not limited to race, class, ethnic, cultural backgrounds and gender. Additionally, the Likert-type items that will compose the SEBEST can be phrased in a positive or negative stance. Figure 2, 2 presents the combinations of these content domains with each cell denoting content that the researcher aimed to represent in the SEBEST." (Ritter, 1999, pp. 36–37)

TRUSTWORTHINESS

Qualitative researchers, in many cases, examine the trustworthiness of their data. Trustworthiness is proven through triangulation of the data, leading the researcher to make claims for the data's credibility, transferability, dependability, and confirmability (Guba & Lincoln, 1981). Some studies require multiple measures and observations; the researcher must provide evidence that the data have been triangulated as a means of ensuring the validity of the study.

Triangulation is a qualitative process that tests the consistency of findings garnered through different methods and sources of data, including field notes, artifacts, and transcripts (Sydenstricker-Neto, 1997; Trochim, 2001). Qualitative researchers also have their subjects review transcripts from audio- or videotaped interviews with the subjects, verifying not only the data but the researcher's interpretation of the data (Zepeda, personal communication, May 1, 2005).

Dissertation Example

"Lincoln and Guba (1985) proposed four alternative constructs to ensure the validity of qualitative data analysis (i.e., credibility, transferability, dependability, confirmability). The researcher addressed all four of these constructs by providing the reader with a detailed description of the procedures and results for both credibility and dependability. In addition, the researcher listened to the participants with an empathic ear in order not to bias the conversations. The transferability of this research was not an issue. This study was conducted to reflect services and professionals in Iowa but the same procedures could be used in other states or with other disability populations (i.e., deaf/hard of hearing)." (Blankenship, 2004, p. 128)

RELIABILITY

Reliability indicates the study's ability to be replicated and produce similar results (Heffner, 2004b). When you measure reliability, you provide evidence that the instrument that you are using produces consistent results over time. In addition, you must identify the various methods used to test reliability (Walonick, 2005).

Dissertation Examples

1. "Relationship Attribution Measure (RAM). This measure is designed to look at attributions made by one partner of the other partner's behavior in response to certain hypothetical situations. In the current study, the overall measure and the two subscales demonstrated good reliability (coefficient alpha: RAM-C = .84, RAM-R = .91, for both women and men)." (Fincham & Bradbury, 1992)
2. "Spouse Specific Support Scale (SSSS). This measure is designed to examine the types of support a participant feels he/she receives from his or her partner. The measure demonstrated good reliability in the current study

(coefficient alpha = .93 for both men and women)."
(Culp & Beach, 1998)

3. "Positive and Negative Affect Scale (PANAS). This measure is designed to examine the intensity and frequency
of various positive and negative emotions experienced
by participants. It was initially developed to measure two
factors: positive affectivity and negative affectivity.
These two factors are modestly correlated (range −.12 to
−.23 over time). It has been shown to have adequate reliability over time (range .84 to .90). The overall scale, as
well as the subscales, demonstrated good reliability in
the current study (coefficient 32 alphas = .92, .90 for
women; PA and NA, respectively; .89 and .91 for men;
PA and NA, respectively). (Banawan, 2004, pp. 31–32)"
(Watson, Clark, & Tellegen, 1988)

4. "The embedded case study protocols are described in the
data collection process. The case study protocols include
the rules and guidelines for the data gathering process
(Yin, 1994). Three methods were employed to maintain
reliability. 1) The researcher recognized the potential for
inherent bias as an employee and researcher in USD 411
(Bogdan & Biklen, 1998). To control for this, the researcher's position was clearly stated to participants as
both researcher and employee of USD 411. 2) Using the
constant comparative method, the data were triangulated
between collection methods, comparing data between

and within themes. 3) A rich and detailed description of the methodology was recorded for an audit trail (Merriam, 2001). The study's reliability was further enhanced through consistency in the questions asked for all focus groups and interviews." (Fast, 2005, p. 46)

SUMMARY

In general, there is a summary or conclusion section at the end of chapter 3. Here you describe all the salient points covered in this chapter. Some researchers also suggest what the reader can expect in the next chapter.

Dissertation Examples

1. "This chapter first situated my study within the framework of ethnographic inquiry, which seeks to document the cosmology of a culture (Bishop, 1999, p. 3). In light of the deterritorialized nature of the subject of my study (or that of any other ethnographic fieldworks in this globalized world), I further presented Appadurai's (1991, 1996) cosmopolitan ethnograph, a methodology that embraces a global approach in addition to the traditional localizing strategy employed by ethnographers. After addressing my position as a native ethnographer, the methodological discussion centered around a detailed

account of my ethnographic field/homework as well as the problematics that emerged in the process. The next chapter explores mediascapes during the 2001 Spring Festival." (Ren, 2003, p. 81)

2. "This chapter focused on the organization, inspiration and methodology which informs the process of inquiry that underpins this work (see Figure 1). It is best represented as a synergistic confluence of thought that integrates three central ideas: a body of writing can take the form of a woven tapestry; different contemporary thinkers and philosophers profoundly informed and inspired the creation of this project from its inception; and qualitative research methodologies sometimes converge to serve as an epistemological framework for philosophical inquiry." (Cooper, 2002, p. 47)

3. "A qualitative design was used as a framework for this study discussing the creation of effective linkages between the Figsboro Elementary School Child Study Committee and agencies that serve children and families. The use of action research as the vehicle to create systemic change for the Figsboro Elementary School Child Study Committee is incorporated into this qualitative design framework. Chapter 4 will discuss the results of this study. These results reflect the data collected through the researcher's journal, individual and focus group interviews, and transcriptions and written minutes of Child Study meetings and inservices." (Grandinetti, 1998, p. 42)

Chapter Four

Results

Chapter 4 is the results chapter in the dissertation in many programs. Each university and often even different departments within universities have peculiar norms related to the reporting of results. Some departments, for example, tie results and discussion together. Others require the researcher to report results in scholarly journal format. You should refer to your department's norms. Present the results in this chapter, based on your data analysis, leaving the discussion and interpretation of the results for chapter 5 (Bradley et al., 1994). Take responsibility to indicate the importance and credibility of each result (Patton, 1990). The reader can expect to see a summarization of data based on how you choose to organize this chapter.

INTRODUCTION

Chapter 4 begins with an introduction that states the purpose of the chapter. Depending on departmental norms, this may be followed by a succinct summary stating how the results are organized. The following examples show how some researchers have introduced this chapter.

Dissertation Examples

1. "Chapter IV presents the results from this study. Results are presented in three sections. The first contains information about the empirical sampling distributions of the fit statistics. . . . The second section contains results that relate to the prediction of the scaling corrections. Included are summaries of the multilevel models that were fitted to the data. . . . The third section presents results that relate to the application of the prediction equations to real items." (Hanson, 2004, p. 103)

2. "Five central themes were identified by this study to be common in meaningful learning experiences: (a) risk, (b) awkwardness, (c) fractional sublimation, (d) reconstruction, and (e) growth. . . . The themes and their respective attributes are substantiated by the writings and comments from this study's participants. Some examples of participants' statements are given in this chapter to illustrate their perspectives, and additional examples from the par-

ticipants can be found in Appendix G under the themes and attributes they represent." (Taniguchi, 2004, p. 79)

3. "The previous chapter described the study design and methodology applied in this dissertation for selecting the study sample, linking the methodology to the research questions for the study, matching the measures employed to the study constructs, and testing the strength and nature of the relationship between constructs. . . . Section 5.1 discusses the factor analysis findings of the dissertation in three stages. . . . Stage 2 analyzes the comprehensive factor analysis results for the longitudinal data, controls for and compares these results to conceptual expectations and the yearly panel results. . . . The complete data results from the factor analyses conducted in Stages 1 through 3 are listed in Appendix A." (Adams, 2004, p. 38)

ORGANIZING THE RESULTS CHAPTER

There is a variety of ways to organize the presentation of results. Some researchers feel that the best way to organize results into an understandable format is through the representation of data using pictorial forms such as charts, graphs, and tables (Tufte, 1997). You must ask yourself three important questions as you prepares to report your results: (1) How should you adapt your report of results to meet the needs of your audience? (2) How do you make the distinction between conclusions based on substantive data and those that may appear to be speculative? (3) How do you ensure that your report of results continues to address issues of confidentiality (Silverstein & Sharp, 1997)? Any organizational schema you choose must be clear and logical and must present the results concisely, accurately, and understandably (Brown, 1997). Information regarding response rate and respondent demographics (when relevant) is usually reported first, followed by reporting of results of data analysis for each hypothesis or research question (Baron, 2005).

In fields that emphasize quantitative research, it is common to organize the reporting of results by hypotheses, restating each hypothesis and addressing each hypothesis as a separate subheading in the same order that they were presented in chapter 1 (Poland, 2003). It is also common to organize by experiment or other similar patterns. You may include a section on the differences you discovered in the patterns, indicating how the patterns support or do not support the research questions (Berkowitz, 1997).

In all cases, whether the study used quantitative, qualitative, or mixed methods, follow an organized schema in presenting the results. Summarize the results at the end of each subsection and again at the end of the chapter.

Dissertation Examples

1. "The aim of this analysis is to evaluate the current situation in terms of computer technology integration in Cyprus

elementary schools. In particular through data analysis the study attempts to identify how elementary teachers in Cyprus apply computers in their classroom practices. Moreover, the study attempts to identify the factors that influence teachers in using computer technology in the classroom. The quantitative analysis presented in this Chapter, includes descriptive and inferential statistics. Version 11 of the SPSS statistical package was used to analyze the quantitative data." (Eteokleous, 2004, p. 41)

2. "The results are presented in two major sections. The first represents the analyses that test the general causal model (see Figure 1). Within this section, path analysis methods are used to test the hypotheses that age only indirectly affects information search and quality of decision rationale through its influence on working memory, vocabulary, preference for control in health decision-making, and prior knowledge of cancer diagnosis and treatment. Also in this section is a presentation of a model that has been optimized for the data." (Talbot, 2004, p. 49)

3. "Following a presentation of descriptive data from the ITBS tests and survey samples, the results of the analyses are presented as responses to the nine research questions presented in Chapter 1. A probability level of .10 or less was considered significant on all measures. The research questions are listed below:

   A. Is there a significant difference in the reading achievement of Title 1 students when parents, teachers, and students exhibit the highest compliance with activities on a learning compact and the reading achievement of students where compact partners exhibit less or the least compliance?

B. Does the level of involvement by teachers or by Title I students make a difference in reading achievement?

C. Does the degree of parental involvement with activities on a learning compact make a significant difference in the reading achievement of Title I students?

D. Does the type of parent involvement (home or school) make a significant difference in reading achievement scores?

E. Does parental monitoring of homework significantly impact reading achievement?

F. Does parental reading with students significant impact reading achievement?

G. Does parental monitoring of television viewing significantly impact-reading achievement?

H. Does parental involvement as a school supporter (attends conferences, attends school functions, eats lunch with child) significantly impact reading achievement?

I. Does parent involvement as a school volunteer (classroom helper, preparation of materials, other volunteer activities) significantly impact reading achievement?

Additionally, qualitative data were derived from parents' answers on two open-ended statements: (1) my goal for my child is_____ (2) If I were in charge of the school I would change my child's education by _____. The results of the two questions will be presented in the final section of this chapter." (Smith, 1998, pp. 50–51)

METHODOLOGY SUMMARY

In this section, remind the reader of the methodology used in completing the study. Summarize your methodology. Make sure the summary of your methodology is consistent with what you previously reported.

Dissertation Examples

1. "This study began in February 2002, with a convenience sample of five classrooms whose teachers volunteered to be a part of the study. The heterogeneous classrooms are located in two elementary schools in the same school district. The school district is located 70 miles north-north-west of New York City. A naturalistic approach was taken by gathering information through classroom observations and by sharing with the teachers after each observation the information was gathered. Quantitative data were obtained from the Grade-4 Science Program Evaluation Test (PET). Data were collected onsite at three different times. Data found on the Classroom Spatial Utilization Form and a

map of each classroom was prepared while visiting each classroom after regular school hours. Classroom observations were conducted during March and April to collect data recorded on the Classroom Migration Form. The Grade-4 Science PET was administered in May 2002." (Duncanson, 2003, p. 109)

2. "In the first experiment, it was shown that articulatory suppression effects are differentiated from irrelevant sound effects (speech and non speech) according to the influence they have on neural processing during a working memory task. An intriguing aspect of the time course data was that these differences appeared at distinct stages of the trial, with articulatory suppression effects emerging within the working memory network very early in the trial (during encoding), and irrelevant sound effects emerging later in the trial (as delay-based processing sets in). These temporal differences suggest a novel behavioral method for dissociating the effects of suppression and irrelevant sound by manipulating the specific timing of irrelevant information during the trial (e.g., by limiting irrelevant information to encoding only, delay only, or retrieval only). Accordingly, the main goal of the second experiment was to explore whether articulatory suppression and irrelevant sounds have different consequences to behavior when limited temporally to a particular stage of the working memory task trial." (Chein, 2004, p. 56)

POPULATION, SAMPLE, AND PARTICIPANTS

If your research used human subjects, describe the subjects, the source of subjects, the selection process used to include or exclude subjects in the study, the number of subjects, and the criteria for selection (Columbia University School of Nursing, 2003). This section is followed by a report of the results for each research question or hypothesis (Baron, 2005).

Dissertation Example

"Research hypothesis 2: The students' perceptions of feedback effectiveness, as reflected by their scores on the Feedback Effectiveness Survey (Appendix E, page 169), are significantly higher during the intervention periods, B1 and B2, than during the baseline periods, A1 and A2. A General Linear Model Repeated Measures procedure reflects temporal differences ($? = .05$). The univariate test for period-related differences on the dependent variable Feedback Effect (Table 4) provided disconfirming results; contrary to Hypothesis 2, the means of the Feedback Effect did not significantly vary by period." (Waddell, 2004, p. 85)

RESULTS

This is the section in which you present your results. The results are shown for the specific research questions or hypotheses (Murtagh & Sterzl, 1995) and are reported accurately without adding interpretation. Make every effort to present the results as accurately and precisely as possible and understand the ethical ramifications related to the reporting of results. Naturally, you must present your results consistent within the norms of your discipline and academic department. Some disciplines, for example, may require results to be reported using the American Psychological Association (2001) guidelines, while other disciplines may require use of *The Chicago Manual of Style* (University of Chicago Press, 2003). The size of the results section will vary according to the research design and methodological approach. There is no one "correct" format for organizing chapter 4.

If you use quantitative data, describe the data and the treatment of the data. Report the data in sufficient detail to justify your conclusions. Some researchers suggest using charts, figures, and tables to clarify the data and to economize on space (Karchmer & Johnson, 1996).

In dissertations using qualitative methods, Miles and Huberman (1994) suggest that results be presented using descriptive and organized text associated with graphic organizers such as matrices.

Dissertation Example

"The results from the adult hobbyists suggested that there were some patterns that might be useful in classrooms, but I suspected that adults might have different types of satisfactions than do high school students. The school culture could also affect the kinds of satisfactions that students take from their work and play. Another concern with the first survey was the possibility that something in the wording of the examples skewed the results. To eliminate these concerns a revised survey for high school students used examples drawn from hobbyists' comments on the previous survey. The extrinsic motivator 'be better than others' included this example: 'Off road motorcycle riding: I hate to admit it, but yes I do really like that I am good at riding, better than most others. It does add to my enjoyment.'" (Pfaffman, 2003, p. 22)

SUMMARY OF RESULTS

In this section, you will present an overall summary of the results, conveying to the reader your salient findings.

Dissertation Examples

1. "Here is a summary of OCAI findings across unique subcultures found: HQMUSE (university headquarters) OCAI data (n = 19 returned surveys with good data of 38 mailed or 50% return rate) reveals a dominant hierarchy type. The aggregate scores for each 'now' and 'preferred' culture types were: clan (26/36); adhocracy (14/17); market (27/27); and hierarchy (32/27). This was

the only subculture of the sixteen examined that rated ad-hocracy as the lowest type in both now and preferred categories. In addition, this was the only subunit that rated hierarchy as both present and somewhat desirable (statistically significant, $p < .05$). All of the other subunits rated hierarchy as least preferred." (Paparone, 2003, p. 90)

2. "In conclusion, aggregate analyses of the final sample data provided some significant results that will in turn assist in the further understanding of the pharmacist-patient relationship. An exploratory common factor analysis was useful in analyzing survey item 2 in order to answer RQ1. Three primary pharmacist roles were identified: 1) traditional role, 2) health care provider role, and 3) alternative therapy source role. Key characteristics and expectations inherent in each role were also noted according to the strength of their loadings. Survey item 7 was examined via correlation analyses and independent samples T-tests in order to explore RQ2. While more research will be necessary in order to fully understand the influence safety issues may have on pharmacist-patient interactions, however both respondent groups agreed upon the basic premise that patients should talk to health care providers when experiencing difficulties with medications and/or new therapies. Finally, frequencies were calculated on survey item 9 to explore the perceived credibility of various health information sources and technologies as questions by RQ3. As expected, pharmacists were perceived to

be credible information sources whereas the Internet is questionable, according to patient responses. Overall, further research will be necessary in order to adequately assess RQ2 and RQ3." (Gade, 2003, p. 61)

SUMMARY AND TRANSITION TO CHAPTER 5

In some dissertations, the researcher may summarize the results as above and include a transition to chapter 5. The transition is included at the end of the summary and introduces the focus of the forthcoming chapter.

Dissertation Example

"In summary, this chapter described some of the participant's experiences within the Youth Partnership Project. The data analysis provided insight to the participant's experiences through their understanding of the project and its process; participants' perspective of their experiences within the project; strategies used within the project; and meaning developed from their experiences within the project. The questions that guided the study were: 1. How do youth and adults who are engaged in developing a sustainable development plan describe their experience within the process of the project? 2. What role does the implementation of a collaborative method play in enhancing civic engagement involving both youth and adults, if any? The final chapter will address the above questions that assisted me in exploring elements within the process of civic engagement. The chapter will also speak to insights constructed from the literature review, as well as contributions of the study and possible future research needs based on the findings of study or information not found within the study." (Reno, 2003, pp. 95–96)

Chapter Five

Interpretation and Recommendations

In chapter 5, depending on departmental norms, you should discuss the interpretation and implications of the results, the relationship to the research questions or hypotheses, the influence of the results on relevant theory or praxis, and the strengths, weaknesses, and limitations of the study (Bartness, 1999). You may also make recommendations for future research (Poland, 2003). Chapter 5 gives you an opportunity to prove the "so what?" question related to the study's significance, providing justification that your study is an important contribution to new knowledge and influencing practice. In essence, chapter 5 allows you to make significant conclusions about your results (Colorado State University, 2001).

INTRODUCTION

There are numerous possible organizational patterns for chapter 5. The organization of this chapter generally follows your academic or department norms. Some dissertations begin with an introduction that provides an overview of the study. In the introduction, briefly restate the problem statement, salient theoretical perspectives, methodology, and results. Then present the reader with an overview of the organization of chapter 5, providing the basic components found in the chapter (Baron, 2005).

Make your final decision regarding chapter organization based on departmental norms. In general, if these require you to restate the purpose of the study, research questions or hypotheses, summary of the conceptual framework, and summary of the literature review, your work is taken from previous chapters. Incorporate your work in the appropriate place in your organizational schema for this chapter (refer to the table of contents or index for reference).

Dissertation Examples

1. "Borderline psychopathology in mothers may negatively impact parenting quality and child development. Problems with chronic emotion deregulation may cause parent sat times to express more hostility or anxiety, towards children, to be emotionally labile, or show an absence of

positive involvement. Borderline psychopathology may create difficulties for parents in regulating appropriate boundaries with children, or being consistent in limit-setting and provision of nurturance. In turn, children may show disturbances in their development, such as behavior problems, insecurity about their self worth, and problems in regulating their own affect." (Barends, 2001, p. 73)

2. "In this final chapter, I pull together a few conclusions, study limitations, and provide some implications for future research. I start with three conclusions I derived from my study that include: 1) how educating culturally competent, reflective practitioners connects the American Physical Therapy profession's historical agenda to American society's changing demographics; 2) integrating cultural competence and reflective practice concepts in physical therapy education requires curricular reform that is a developmental process necessitating transformative leadership, adaptive work, significant reflection, and long-term commitment that results in changed behaviors of faculty and students; and 3) the need for explicit curriculum that emphasizes culture and reflective practice. I follow my conclusions by presenting implications for future research." (Romanello, 2001, p. 191)

3. "As described in Chapter 1, I designed this research project to begin identifying the components of teacher interest and to explore how teacher interest affects student interest in a subject. By examining the interaction between

teacher interest and student subject interest in two core s
(social studies and English) where student attendance was
required, I focused on the teacher's role in influencing
student subject interest. This information was especially
important because a relationship of interest represents
positive value for the person who is pursuing the object.
Therefore, teachers and students who actively pursue a
subject of interest can expect to derive benefit from their
connections with the subject. The research questions developed to explore the process of connecting with the
content are restated below." (Long, 2003, p. 157)

SUMMARY OF RESULTS

In this section, you will summarize the results you identified
in the previous chapter. You may list the results as a group and
then discuss each result separately, or list a single result, discuss it, and repeat the process for each of the remaining results.

Dissertation Examples

1. "The present study focused on questions regarding ethnicity, level of religiosity, remorse, and forgiveness.
   Analyses related to hypothesis one examined possible
   ethnicity differences for all major variables. As expected,
   there were differences found among African Americans
   and Caucasians related to religiosity, providing support

for the first hypothesis. Here, African Americans tended to report higher levels of religiosity (partner) than their Caucasian counterparts and that they attended religious services more often during the past year than did Caucasians (self and partner). This is not surprising given past research that reports that African Americans have a strong religious orientation overall and tend to be more religious than the general population (Taylor, Chatters, Jayakody, & Levin, 1996)." (Bedell, 2002, p. 76)

2. "No support emerged from the current study for any of our four hypotheses. First, the study provided no support for the hypothesis that overly positive self-perceptions and aggressive behavior would be positively associated cross-sectionally. Second, the study provided no support for the hypothesis that the relation between overly positive self perceptions and aggression increases as children progress through adolescence. Third, the results provided no support for the hypothesis that overly positive self-perceptions predict later aggressive behavior. Finally, the results of the current study provided no support for the notion that aggressive behavior predicts later levels of overly positive self-perceptions." (Hoffman, 2003, p. 44)

DISCUSSION OF RESULTS

In the discussion section, you will go beyond the evidence you presented in chapter 4 by providing the rationale for the

results, interpreting and explaining your conclusions. Moreover, you can expound on your insights on the effect of your
work on established theory (Murtagh & Sterzl, 1995; Skelton & Edwards, 2000) by including salient literature and
studies examined in chapter 2, the review of the literature.

Dissertation Examples

1. "In this study, the results of Social Integration and Greek
   Affiliation seemed to run parallel. This is unsurprising,
   since Greek Affiliation can be considered a possible factor in Social Integration. At the same time, only Greek
   Predisposition appears to have a significant influence on
   Mature Interpersonal Relationship. It seems surprising
   that Social Integration had no influence on Mature Interpersonal Relationship when previous studies had shown
   that intimate relationships, campus organizations, and
   extracurricular activities had all appeared to have significant influence on developing Mature Interpersonal Relationships (Erwin and Love, 1989; Hood, 1984; and Ri-
   ahinejad and Hood, 1984). However, it is possible that
   there were simply not enough opportunities beyond the
   students' freshman year for higher-order challenges to
   produce sufficient growth (Hagedorn, Pacarella, Edison,
   Braxton, Nora, & Terenzini, 1999). Another way to view
   it is that although social integration occurs mainly in the
   first year of college, it is insufficient in and of itself to

further the development of Mature Interpersonal Relationships (Hagedorn, Pacarella, Edison, Braxton, Nora, & Terenzini, 1999). As Rogers (1980) and Stage (1991) have suggested, further growth in psychosocial development may require higher-order challenges, such as study abroad, or greater support for students throughout their college careers." (Lien, 2002, p. 44)

2. "The implications of this study's findings are important for families, schools, and larger communities. Millions of dollars are being spent each year trying to determine the root causes and cures for social ills, yet with seemingly little success in many cases. I believe that our continued failures at societal reform are the result of the same 'bigger and better' approach noted by Torrance (1979) in which 'new' solutions are not really new, they are simply bigger and more expensive versions of the same tired schemes that have always failed before." (Kyzer, 2001, pp. 245–246)

SUMMARY STATEMENT

This section summarizes the results and draws conclusions. You may find this format particularly useful when you discuss each result separately. When using a conclusion section at the end of the entire discussion section, restate the significance of your study and speculate about the next steps toward further research. In this section, indicate that your study alerts the reader to new questions emanating from your research (Brown, 1997).

Dissertation Examples

1. "Several conclusions can be drawn from this study that deserves consideration with respect to undergraduate science education and the larger science education community in general. As with any first look at a curriculum, this study also raises questions that deserve further investigation. This section addresses conclusions that have been made after reflection on the completed research and poses directions for further study." (McKenzie, 1996, p. 135)

2. "This study represents one of the most comprehensive to date, measuring agreement, using multiple methods, among more than 38,000 incumbents in 61 occupational series and 261 series grades. As predicted, agreement failed to reach acceptable levels in nearly every case. However, contrary to expectation, experience, occupational complexity, and KSAO abstractness accounted for little of the disagreement. Although the reasons for these null findings are not entirely clear, the most likely explanation is that true cross-position variance simply overshadowed the variance due to these rater, occupation, and item characteristics. If so, then the disagreement reported here reflects a coarse classification system that inadequately distinguishes among meaningful subgroups within single occu-

pational titles. The existence of such subgroups threatens not so much the predictive validity of job specifications as their content validity, in so far as predictive KSAOs are not identified as such. Future research must focus on the existence of such subgroups, their consequences, and ways of identifying them." (Bumkrant, 2003, p. 74)

IMPLICATIONS FOR FURTHER RESEARCH

In this section, discuss how your study instructs future research. Clearly state the connections to future research so others can benefit and extrapolate your theoretical perspectives or research design to extend their research (Colorado State University, 2001). Making suggestions for further research forces you to examine your research critically and to identify improvements in further applications of your research design. You may indicate whether the topic you studied warrants additional inquiry and, if so, suggest the design for such a study. In addition, examine the complementary nature of your research with other research in the field and suggest future areas of inquiry (International University of Professional Studies, 2004).

Dissertation Examples

1. "Additional qualitative studies regarding community college scholarship are warranted, I believe. While some of

my findings are in concert with the findings of researchers like James Palmer, I find great value in looking at the issues related to faculty scholarship from an emic perspective. This treatment leads to a different, perhaps richer understanding of the nature of community college scholarship than has been presented in the literature." (Kelly-Kleese, 2001, p. 142)

2. "Using techniques similar to those utilized in this study it would be possible to perform analyses of other governmental programs to determine if performance-based initiatives were having impact in other areas. . . . Again depending upon the availability of data, programs funding higher education could be analyzed in other states. Finally, additional work could be done . . . to see if other measures not considered in this study were negatively impacted during the duration of the performance-based funding system. Did community programs suffer? Did the quality of graduates entering the state university system decline? Was access to the institutions decreased for at-risk populations that would be less likely to achieve the desired outcomes?" (Phillips, 2002, p. 69)

IMPLICATIONS FOR PRACTICE AND RECOMMENDATIONS

Here, discuss how your results contribute to practice, answering the question of the implications of your study for changing the way people think about practice (Brown, 1997). You have the opportunity to speculate as to the potential real-world impact of your results (Bradley et al., 1994). Your discussion, although speculative, should present a rational approach to the impact of the study's results (Skelton & Edwards, 2000). In any event, be careful to make sure the reader understands that this is speculation and does not convey an unsubstantiated set of results. In some professional fields, researchers do not speak to practice but rather to recommendations for specific actions that may be related to policy or other pertinent areas (Baron, 2005).

Dissertation Examples

1. "As Polio (2003) points out, there are very few qualitative studies in second language research, and of those, even fewer are naturalistic inquiry. If descriptive studies are instructive rather than prescriptive (Macbeth, 2004) and if, as Gallas (1998) believes, understanding must precede prescription, then it would seem that the field could benefit from more naturalistic inquiry. Second language writing for graduate students who are cultural strangers has been taken up more enthusiastically (e.g., Belcher, 1989; Brandt, 1992; Casanave, 1995; Fox, 1991; Prior, 1995) than interest in 'ordinary worlds' of basic, or entry level, cultural strangers. In the literature, there is a marked preference for programs of curricular or instructional engineering. . . . Although these studies are

clearly interested in socio-cultural influences, those influences are usually regarded as formal mechanisms in broad macro-cultural (and thus cognitive) terms. A case based program of naturalistic inquiry yielding tutorials for practitioners would proceed in a very different fashion." (Macbeth, 2004, p. 220)

2. "The implications are directed toward the 4-H professionals in the North Carolina Cooperative Extension Service. The implications may also have utility with the 4-H profession nationally and the North Carolina Cooperative Extension Service Personal and Organization Development system, for validation of the competencies. The following were considered to be the most significant implications." (Burke, 2002, pp. 99–100)

3. "The most relevant example from this research for developing online communities of museum educators and teachers is the notion of an online community of practice. This could be structured as one section of a larger educational museum web site with several different areas. Allowing participants to choose and easily access the areas of the discussion that are relevant for them is essential. It is important to have a mix of teachers and museum educators as peripheral participants and as full participants. Additionally, instead of having the policies related to who can post to the community dominated by institutional fear of inappropriate content, it is important to allow the community members access to post information

and to allow the community as a group to censure any inappropriate content." (Buffington, 2004, p. 217)

RELATIONSHIP OF RESULTS TO THEORY

Your efforts in this section to connect the results to existing theory are a way of integrating the chapters of the dissertation. Having introduced theory in chapter 1 (in the problem statement and the significance of the study), expanded the notion of applicable theory in chapter 2, and linked the theory to the methodology in chapter 3, this section now ties it all together in the discussion of the study's results (Poland, 2003).

Dissertation Example

"The conceptual frameworks for this study were phenomenological theory, social support theory, and health belief model. Fear and anxiety about the disease reflected patterns of phenomenological theory where patients openly shared situations that they had encountered while suffering from chronic hypertensive cardiovascular disease. Consistent with van Manen's (1990) perspective, the patients and caregivers rendered their experiences through story-telling. For example, one patient expressed her fear of becoming too stressed and for fear of having a heart attack or a stroke. . . . A theory as proposed by Harding (1981) states that many African

Americans believe that because they have survived the en-
counter of slavery that they are almost invincible. This health
belief termed 'fatalism' is one of the reasons why there are
African Americans who do not see hypertension as a threat
(Vaughan, 1993). 'Fatalism' is defined as the belief that since
African Americans have been through so much in this country (i.e., slavery, poverty, pain and mental anguish from past
experiences) that hypertension is not perceived as a threat.
Some evidence of this theory was supported by one patient's
comment about her life of trials." (Lang, 2003, p. 94)

LIMITATIONS

In this section, discuss the limitations of your study related
to validity, reliability, credibility, trustworthiness, and other
methodological issues that occurred during the study. The
discussion of limitations occurs in relationship to the limitations that may impede similar studies (Health, 1997) or influence different methodological designs in future studies.

Dissertation Examples

1. "Aside from the commonplace limitations of a qualitative case study, some study-specific limitations also exist. The most apparent limitation within the scope of this
   study was an inability to gather conclusive objective data

for the third year of the existence of the electronic screening system, year 2000. While it is the opinion of the researcher than presenting both subjective and objective data analysis was an innovative approach, it remains that some of the numerical data was incomplete and did not, therefore, yield as conclusive of results as might have otherwise occurred had this study been conducted later in the year. Year-to-date data regarding total number of applicant requisitions sent to the districts, total number of new hires and total number of minority new hires, in particular, remains incomplete since only five months of 2000 data is available (January through May, 2000)." (Lewis, 2000, pp. 170–171)

2. "There were several limitations to this study that restrict the generalization of its results. The results of the present study have been generated by the validation procedure outlined in Chapter 3 during four successive semesters (Fall 1999 to Spring 2001) at the Pennsylvania State University and Arizona State University. The sample consisted of sophomore to graduate level students enrolled in modern physics, undergraduate quantum mechanics, graduate quantum mechanics, and graduate chemistry quantum mechanics courses. The sample size was 146 students in all groups combined. Ideally, more students should be involved in a validation study (Nunnally, 1978). Due to the nature of the concepts and the unique population, it would have been extremely difficult to administer

several iterations to hundreds of students as recommended by some experts. Due to the small sample size and due to the limited number of universities involved in the study, however, caution is warranted in interpreting results, especially in Chapter 4 section 4.5 a–e. While the students who have participated in this study were most likely representative of groups in similar universities, caution is warranted in applying these findings to other populations since, for example, the students were predominantly male. . . . Data gathered in this validation study were gathered principally from volunteers whose final course grades were not based upon their performance on the QMVI." (Cataloglu, 2002, pp. 117–118)

SUMMARY AND CONCLUSION

Each dissertation ends with a conclusion that is a comprehensive summative statement of the researcher's study. Depending on department norms, you may refer to this section as the summary or the conclusion. In this section, highlight the salient features of your dissertation and, if desired, suggest ideas for future research (London South Bank University, 2004). This section offers you an opportunity to state your perspective.

Dissertation Examples

1. "Social movements have become an increasingly prevalent aspect of American society (Macionis, 1995). Organizations have distinguished themselves both by their willingness to respond to these movements and their reluctance to do so. This wide range of responses raises the question, under what conditions do firms respond to social movements? The results of this study suggest that public support and industry attention to the movement facilitate organizational action. Contrary to expectations, direct governmental coercion had little influence over organizations. These results offer several implications for theoretical development. First, they suggest that contrary to conventional assumptions institutional environments are not monolithic in terms of their influence over firms. Different institutional forces appear to exert different pressures on firms. This suggests that institutional environments may be more complex than previously expected. Second, the results failed to support the notion that the government can force action. This suggests that the real power to facilitate organizational action and social change may lie in public acceptance and visibility of social concerns. These findings provide the basis for future examinations and explanations of this complex phenomenon." (Bergh, 2002, pp. 64–65)

2. "In conclusion, this study was an attempt to investigate the dynamic socialization process using a more comprehensive cognition, affect, behavior framework and by testing longitudinal, mediated relationships. Unidirectional causation and person situation interactions are important, especially for theory development, however research must become more comprehensive as theory becomes more developed. This study has shown that stable individual differences, cognition, affect, and behavior (information seeking and performance behavior) are important in newcomer socialization. They are interdependent and should not necessarily be thought of as outcomes. This study has also shown that socialization patterns appear to generalize to blue-collar workers and part time workers. Although this study failed to provide compelling evidence in support of cyclical recursive relationships, these type of relationships are important, seem highly probable, and require more attention in future research." (Brink, 2003, p. 104)

Appendix

Advice on References and Plagiarism

REFERENCES

In the reference list, include every reference that you cited in the text, and do not include references not cited in the text (Bartness, 1999). Department norms determine the citation style for the researcher's references. Frequently used stylistic systems are APA (American Psychological Association), MLA (Modern Language Association), and CMS (*Chicago Manual of Style*).

PLAGIARISM

Plagiarism is intellectual theft. "It is using another person's words or ideas without giving credit to the other person. . . .

[Y]ou must put quotation marks around them and give the writer or speaker credit by revealing the source in a citation" (Harris, 2004, para. 5). Researchers make a good faith commitment to give credit to all sources in writing their dissertations. Stress associated with writing the dissertation may tempt a researcher to take intellectual shortcuts, including cutting and pasting another's work. These actions threaten the foundation of academia and erode future credibility. In academia, researchers trust one another as the basis for the pursuit of new knowledge. They share ideas, work, and credit.

Avoiding plagiarism is easy, provided you are willing to give credit where credit is due. Some excellent database software programs make it easy to provide citations. In the following quote, I provide the citation for the quote with the Endnote software program. Since I wrote this book in APA style, quotes more than 40 words are blocked without using quotation marks, as follows:

> You cite your sources to give credit to those people whose ideas/words you are using in your paper and to distinguish their ideas/words from your own ideas and words; to make your argument stronger. Doing research on an issue strengthens your position, because it shows you have engaged with some of the other positions on your topic and incorporated them into your thinking; to allow your readers to verify your claims and to get more information from the source materials. (Emory University Libraries, 2004, para. 1)

QUOTING, PARAPHRASING, AND SUMMARIZING

Here is a heuristic when writing your dissertation: when quoting, make sure the quote is accurate. Use quotation marks or another appropriate format form (depending on the department norms for the style guide) that indicate the material is a quote.

> Use direct quotations only when the author's wording is necessary or particularly effective. If you are using material cited by an author and you do not have the original source, introduce the quotation with a phrase such as "as quoted in . . ." Place all direct quotations within quotation marks, or indent them if using block quotes. Be sure to copy quotations exactly as they appear. (Revere, 2004)

When you paraphrase, you adapt the source material into your words and sentence structure, providing a citation for the source of the information. Use your words but precisely convey the author's ideas and meaning. Give credit to the author in a citation (Morgan, 2004; Indiana University, 2004).

A summary is generally shorter than paraphrasing, but the source of the summary must also be cited (Purdue University, 2001). The bottom line for researchers is: When in doubt, cite!

References

Adams, E. H. (2002). *Community-based programming: Perceived levels of utility, practice, and encouragement among North Carolina Community College mid-level managers.* Unpublished EdD, North Carolina State University, Raleigh, NC.

Adams, G. (2004). *Power plays: A longitudinal examination of CEO/BOD power circulation and its impact on organizational performance.* Unpublished PhD, Florida State University, Tallahassee, FL.

Afolabi, M. (1992). The review of related literature. *International Journal of Information and Library, 4*(1), 59–66.

Akbulut, A. (2003). *An investigation of the factors that influence electronic information sharing between state and local agencies.* Unpublished PhD, Louisiana State University, Baton Rouge, LA.

Ali-Dinar, Ali B., ed. (n.d.). *Components of a dissertation proposal.* University of Pennsylvania, African Studies Center. Retrieved on January 17, 2005, from http://www.africa.upenn.edu/Acad_Research/etien_comp.html.

Allgood, J. (2003). *Initiation of treatment for alcohol abuse: A developmental approach.* Unpublished PhD, Florida State University, Tallahassee, FL.

Alzate, M. (2002). *The quality of life of single mothers on welfare in Georgia and the 1996 welfare reform.* Unpublished PhD, University of Georgia, Athens, GA.

American Psychological Association. (2001). *Publication manual of the American Psychological Association* (5th ed.). Washington, DC: American Psychological Association.

Ammon, S. C. (2002). *Global economics, domestic politics, and reforms of social insurance programs in advanced capitalist countries.* Unpublished PhD, Nashville, TN, Knoxville, KY.

Anderson, A. (2003). *A descriptive study of the criteria used for school choice selection and preference among African American parents/caregivers in an integrated magnet school district of choice.* Unpublished EdD, Seton Hall University, South Orange, NJ.

Andre, P., Bitondo, D., Berthelot, M., & Louillet, D. (2001). *Development of a conceptual and methodological frameworks for the integrated assessment of the impacts of linear infrastructure projects on quality of life.* Retrieved on February 17, 2005, from http://www.ceaa-acee.gc.ca/015/0002/0015/5_e.htm.

Babbie, E. (2001). *The practice of social research* (9th ed.). Belmont, CA: Wadsworth.

Baehr, A. (2004). *Wounded healers and relational experts: A grounded theory of experienced psychotherapists' management and use of counter transference.* Unpublished PhD, Pennsylvania State University, University Park, PA.

Bailey, K. (2002). *The effects of learning strategies on student interaction and student satisfaction.* Unpublished PhD, Pennsylvania State University, University Park, PA.

Baker, D. (2001). *The evaluation of university-community engagement scholarship within the college level promotion and tenure process.* Unpublished PhD, Virginia Polytechnic Institute and State University, Blacksburg, VA.

Barends, N. (2001). *Maternal borderline personality characteristics and family functioning.* Unpublished PhD, Pennsylvania State University, University Park, PA.

Baron, M. (2005). *Guidelines for writing research proposals and dissertations.* Retrieved on May 12, 2005, from http://www.usd.edu/ahed/quantguide.cfm.

Bartness, T. (1999). *Department of Psychology dissertation guidelines.* Retrieved on May 12, 2005, from http://www.gsu.edu/psychology/PsycDeptDissertationGuidelines.doc.

Bath, A. (2002). *The relationship between person-environment congruence and fundamental goals for African American and European American, female college students.* Unpublished PhD, Ohio State University, Columbus, OH.

Bedell, T. (2002). *The role of religiosity in forgiveness.* Unpublished PhD, Ohio State University, Columbus, OH.

Beloney-Morrison, T. (2003). *Your blues ain't like mine: Exploring the promotion and tenure process of African American female professors at select research universities in the South.* Unpublished PhD, Louisiana State University, Baton Rouge, LA.

Bergh, J. (2002). *Do social movements matter to organizations? An institutional theory perspective on corporate responses to the contemporary environmental movement.* Unpublished PhD, Pennsylvania State University, University Park, PA.

Berkowitz, S. (1997). *Chapter 4: Analyzing qualitative data.* Retrieved from http://www.ehr.nsf.gov/EHR/REC/pubs/NSF97-153/CHAP_4.HTM.

Blankenship, K. (2004). *Looking for success: Transition planning for students with visual impairments in the State of Iowa.* Unpublished PhD, Vanderbilt University, Nashville, TN.

Bodur, Y. (2003). *Preservice teachers' learning of multiculturalism in a teacher education program.* Unpublished PhD, Florida State University, Tallahassee, FL.

Bond, C. (2004). *Does increasing Black homeownership decrease residential segregation?* Unpublished PhD, University of Notre Dame, South Bend, IN.

Bondima, M. H. (2004). *The nature of culturally responsive pedagogy in two urban African American middle school science classrooms.* Unpublished PhD, University of Maryland College Park, University Park, MD.

Boyd, F. (2000). *Non-verbal behaviors of effective teachers of at-risk African-American male middle school students.* Unpublished EdD, Virginia Polytechnic Institute and State University, Blacksburg, VA.

Bradley, L., Flathouse, P., Gould, L., Hendricks, C., & Robinson, B. (1994). *The basics of dissertation writing.* Retrieved on October 19, 2004, from http://www.bamaed.ua.edu/~kcarmich/WRITING.KDC.htm.

Brink, K. (2003). *New hire socialization: The dynamic relationships among individual differences, cognition, affect, and behavior.* Unpublished PhD, University of Georgia, Athens, GA.

Brown, H. (1997). *Writing your dissertation.* Retrieved on December 6, 2004, from http://www.educ.hku.hk/student/maual/dissert2.htm#step3.

Buffington, M. (2004). *Using the Internet to develop students' critical thinking skills and build online communities of teachers: A review of research with implications for museum education.* Unpublished PhD, Ohio State University, Columbus, OH.

Bumkrant, S. (2003). *Interrater agreement of incumbent job specification importance ratings: Rater, occupation, and item effects* (PhD). Blacksburg, VA: Virginia Polytechnic Institute and State University.

Burke, T. (2002). *Defining competency and reviewing factors that may impact knowledge perceived importance and use of competence in the 4-H professional's job.* Unpublished PhD, North Carolina State University, Raleigh, NC.

Cain, S. (2003). *A comparison of community members preference to viewing two different approaches to therapy.* Unpublished PhD, West Virginia University, Morgantown, WV.

Calabrese, R., Sheppard, D., Hummel, C., Laramore, C., & Nance, E. (2005). *Identifying teachers' and administrators' perceptions of the efficacy of the impact of professional development on the quality of teacher instruction.* Wichita, KS: Wichita State University.

Calabrese, R., Sherwood, K., Fast, J., & Womack, C. (2003). *Pay for performance plans in selected school districts: A systematic literature review.* Wichita, KS: Wichita State University.

Capacci-Carneal, C. (2004). *Community schools in Mali: A multilevel analysis.* Unpublished PhD, Florida State University, Tallahassee, FL.

Carper, A. (2002). *Bright students in a wasteland: The at-risk gifted, a qualitative study of fourteen gifted dropouts.* Unpublished EdD, North Carolina State University, Raleigh, NC.

Carpiniello, K. (2004). *The development of adolescent panic, depression, and alcohol expectancies as a function of anxiety sensitivity.* Unpublished PhD, Fordham University, New York, NY.

Cataloglu, E. (2002). *Development and validation of an achievement test in introductory quantum mechanics: The quantum mechanics visualization instrument (QMVI).* Unpublished PhD, Pennsylvania State University, University Park, PA.

Charlton, R. (1986). *The effects of environmental and system variables on school grade organization (Massachusetts).* Unpublished EdD, Northeastern University, Boston, MA.

Chein, J. (2004). *Evaluating models of working memory: FMRI and behavioral evidence on the effects of concurrent irrelevant information.* Unpublished PhD, University of Pittsburgh, Pittsburgh, PA.

Clark, D., Guba, E., & Smith, G. (1977). *Functions and definitions of a research proposal.*

Collins, J. (2004). *Adult and community college education.* Unpublished PhD, North Carolina State University, Raleigh, NC.

Colorado State University. (2001). *Dissertation guide.* School of Education. Retrieved on December 7, 2004, from http://soe-grad.colostate.edu/pubs/DissertationGuide.pdf.

Columbia University School of Nursing. (2003). *Doctor of nursing science program student handbook.* New York: Columbia University.

Cooper, E. (2002). *Living in the question: An inward journey to the heart of the practice of inquiry.* Unpublished EdD, University of Cincinnati, Cincinnati, OH.

Cooper, H. M. (1988). The structure of knowledge synthesis. *Knowledge in Society, 1*, 104–126.

Crotogino, J. (2002). *Visual stress in migraine: Subjective and psychophysiological responses to intense visual stimulation.* Unpublished PhD, McGill University, Montreal, Canada.

Dallal, G. (2004). *Units of analysis.* Retrieved on May 13, 2005, from http://www.tufts.edu/~gdallal/units.htm.

D'Angelo, P. (2002). *CA 5000 communication research: Proposal assignments.* Retrieved on May 8, 2005, from http://www16.homepage.villanova.edu/paul.dangelo/comm5000/Proposal%20Assignments.htm.

DeGraaf, D. (1992). *The relationship between selected individual variables as they relate to camp counselors' ranking of work motivators.* Unpublished PhD, University of Oregon, Eugene, OR.

DeMarzo, J. (1998). *Sexual knowledge, attitudes and behaviors of an ethnically diverse sample of community college students in metropolitan New York.* Unpublished EdD, Teachers College, Columbia University, New York, NY.

DeWitz, S. J. (2004). *Exploring the relationship between self-efficacy beliefs and purpose in life.* Unpublished PhD, Ohio State University, Columbus, OH.

Duncanson, E. (2003). *The impact of classroom organization in grade 4 on student achievement in science.* Unpublished EdD, Seton Hall University, South Orange, NJ.

Durand, R. E. (2004). *The effects of an interdisciplinary project on student learning of natural selection.* Unpublished MA, California State University Fullerton, Fullerton, CA.

Emory University Libraries. (2004). *Citing your sources and plagiarism*, part 4, *Citation styles and citing sources.* Retrieved on April 24, 2005, from http://web.library.emory.edu/services/ressvcs/citation/plagiarismpart4.html#whycite.

Eteokleous, N. (2004). *Computer technology integration in Cyprus elementary schools.* Unpublished PhD, Pennsylvania State University, University Park, PA.

Fast, J. (2005). *A study of the aspirations of the Goessel Unified School District, USD 411.* Unpublished EdD, Wichita State University, Wichita, KS.

Feldman, D. (2003). What are we talking about when we talk about theory? *Journal of Management, 30*(5).

Franco, W. (2003). *Hydrodynamics and control in thermal-fluid networks.* Unpublished PhD, University of Notre Dame, South Bend, IN.

Gade, C. J. (2003). *An exploration of the pharmacist-patient communicative relationship.* Unpublished PhD, Ohio State University, Columbus, OH.

Gage, C. Q. (2003). *The meaning and measure of school mindfulness: An exploratory analysis.* Unpublished PhD, Ohio State University, Columbus, OH.

Gaines, J. (2001). *Worry and associated symptoms in younger versus middle-aged adults with DSM-IV generalized anxiety disorder at pre- and post-treatment.* Unpublished PhD, Pennsylvania State University, University Park, PA.

Georgia Institute of Technology. (2001). *Scientific approaches for transportation research*. School of Civil and Environmental Engineering. Retrieved on January 20, 2005, from http://traffic.ce .gatech.edu/nchrp2045/v1chapter5.html.

Gerda, J. J. (2004). *A history of the conferences of deans of women, 1903–1922.* Unpublished PhD, Bowling Green State University, Bowling Green, OH.

Ginorio, A. (n.d.). *The scientific method: A model for conducting scientific research*. Retrieved on February 9, 2005, from http:// depts.washington.edu/rural/RURAL/design/scimethod.html.

Glatthorn, A. (1998). *Writing the winning dissertation*. Thousand Oaks, CA: Corwin Press.

Godfrey, P. (2003). *Listening to students' and teachers' voices: An ecological case study investigating the transition from elementary to middle school.* Unpublished PhD, North Carolina State University, Raleigh, NC.

Gohn, J. (2004). *Signs of change: The role of team leadership and culture in science education reform.* Unpublished PhD, Miami University, Oxford, OH.

Gossett, J. (2002). *Economic development and community colleges: Attributes, attitudes and satisfaction levels of western North Carolina stakeholders.* Unpublished EdD, North Carolina State University, Raleigh, NC.

Gradwell, S. (2004). *Communicating planned change: A case study of leadership credibility.* Unpublished PhD, Drexel University, Philadelphia, PA.

Grandinetti, P. (1998). *Developing collaboration between the Figsboro Elementary School Child Study Committee and agencies that serve children and families.* Unpublished EdD, Virginia Polytechnic Institute and State University, Blacksburg, VA.

Guba, E., & Lincoln, Y. (1981). *Effective evaluation: Improving the usefulness of evaluation results through responsive and naturalistic approaches.* San Francisco, CA: Jossey-Bass.

Hakuta, K. (1990). Bilingualism and bilingual education: A research perspective. *Occasional Papers in Bilingual Education* (1).

Hanson, M. A. (2004). *Predicting the distribution of a goodness-of-fit statistic appropriate for use with performance-based assessments.* Unpublished PhD, University of Pittsburgh, Pittsburgh, PA.

Harris, R. (2004). *Anti-plagiarism strategies for research papers.* Retrieved on May 3, 2005, from http://www.virtualsalt.com/antiplag.htm.

Health, A. (1997). The proposal in qualitative research. *Qualitative Report, 3*(1).

Heffner, C. (2004a). *Research Methods.* Retrieved on April 19, 2005, from http://allpsych.com/researchmethods/index.html.

Heffner, C. (2004b). *Test validity and reliability.* Retrieved on December 4, 2004, from http://allpsych.com/researchmethods/validityreliability.html.

Helberg, C. (1996). Pitfalls of data analysis. *Research & Evaluation, 5*(5).

Hoffman, K. (2003). *The "dark side" of self esteem: Examining the relation between overly-positive self-perceptions and aggressive behavior in adolescents.* Unpublished PhD, University of Notre Dame, South Bend, IN.

Hollist, C. (2002). *Marital satisfaction and depression in a study of Brazilian women: A cross-cultural test of the marital discord model of depression.* Unpublished PhD, Brigham Young University, Salt Lake City, UT.

Horak, J. J. (2002). *Factors prediction distress at marital therapy onset.* Unpublished PhD, Western Michigan University, Kalamazoo, MI.

House, C. (2004). *Out and about: Predictors of lesbians' outness in the workplace.* Unpublished PhD, Pennsylvania State University, University Park, PA.

Hsiao-Rai Hsi, S. (1997). *Facilitating knowledge integration in science through electronic discussion: The multimedia forum kiosk.* Unpublished PhD, University of California, Berkeley, CA.

Hutchinson, J. (2004). *Psychological factors in perceived and sustained effort.* Unpublished PhD, Florida State University, Tallahassee, FL.

Indiana University. (2004). *Plagiarism: What it is and how to recognize and avoid it.* Instructional Support Services, Writing Tutorial Services. Retrieved on May 6, 2005, from http://www .indiana.edu/~wts/pamphlets/plagiarism.shtml.

International University of Professional Studies. (2004). *Dissertation Manual.*

Johnson, D. K. (2002). *General education 2000—A national survey: How general education changed between 1989 and 2000.* Unpublished PhD, Pennsylvania State University, University Park, PA.

Johnson, D. M. (2002). *The role of initial coping strategies on subsequent appointment attendance in individuals with HIV: A longitudinal analysis.* Unpublished PhD, Louisiana State University, Baton Rouge, LA.

Johnson, R. B. (2003). *Chapter 3: Problem identification and hypothesis formation.* Retrieved on May 3, 2005, from http://

www.southalabama.edu/coe/bset/johnson/dr_johnson/lectures/
lec3.htm.

Joppe, M. (2004). *The research process*. Retrieved on December
4, 2004, from http://www.ryerson.ca/%7Emjoppe/rp.htm.

Karchmer, M. (1996). *An alternative dissertation research model*.
Retrieved on May 7, 2005, from http://gradschool.gallaudet
.edu/dissertation/appendixl.html.

Karchmer, M., & Johnson, R. (1996). *Dissertation handbook*.
Retrieved on October 15, 2004, from http://gradschool
.gallaudet.edu/dissertation/overview.html.

Keeler, C. (2003). *Developing and using an instrument to describe
instructional design elements of high school online courses*.
Unpublished PhD, University of Oregon, Eugene, OR.

Kelly-Kleese, C. (2001). *Community college scholarship and dis-
course: An intrinsic case study*. Unpublished EdD, North Carolina State University, Raleigh, NC.

Kennedy, I. (2004). *How to do research*. Retrieved on May 7, 2005,
from http://www.geocities.com/Athens/3238/page3-15.htm.

Koopman, P. (1997). *How to write an abstract*. Retrieved on January 12, 2005, from http://www.ece.cmu.edu/~koopman/
essays/abstract.html.

Krumme, G. (2000). *Phases, stages and steps in geographic investigation and research*. Retrieved on September 21, 2004,
from   http://faculty.washington.edu/krumme/guides/re-
searchguide.html.

Krumme, G. (2002). *Economic geography: Toward a conceptual
framework*. Retrieved on May 8, 2005, from http://faculty
.washington.edu/~krumme/gloss/c.html#concept.

Kunder, L. H. (1998). *Employees' perceptions of the status and effectiveness of the training and development system and of the value of training and development.* Unpublished PhD, Virginia Polytechnic Institute and State University, Blacksburg, VA.

Kyzer, M. (2001). *Empathy, creativity, and conflict resolution in adolescents.* Unpublished PhD, University of Georgia, Athens, GA.

Lang, L. (2003). *Expressed coping strategies and techniques among African American families in north Florida who are living with chronic hypertensive cardiovascular disease.* Unpublished PhD, Florida State University, Tallahassee, FL.

LeJeune, E. (2001). *Critical analysis.* Retrieved on May 9, 2005, from http://www.selu.edu/Academics/Faculty/elejeune/critique.htm.

Lewis, R. (2000). *Gatekeeping for children: How the use of an electronic screening process affects teacher selection in a regional education service center in Texas.* Unpublished EdD, Pennsylvania State University, University Park, PA.

Lien, L. (2002). *The role of social integration in students' psychosocial development.* Unpublished PhD, Vanderbilt University, Nashville, TN.

London South Bank University. (2004). *Study skills materials—Dissertations.* Learning Development Centre. Retrieved on May 10, 2005, from http://www.lsbu.ac.uk/caxton/studyskills/materials/dissertations.htm.

Long, J. F. (2003). *Connecting with the content: How teacher interest affects student interest in a core course.* Unpublished PhD, Ohio State University, Columbus, OH.

Luseno, F. K. (2001). *An assessment of the perceptions of secondary special and general education teachers working in inclusive settings in the Commonwealth of Virginia.* Unpublished PhD, Virginia Polytechnic Institute and State University, Blacksburg, VA.

Macbeth, K. (2004). *The situated achievements of novices learning academic writing as a cultural curriculum.* Unpublished PhD, Ohio State University, Columbus, OH.

Mather, M. (2004). *The contextual, academic, and socio-cultural factors influencing kindergarten students' mathematical literacy development.* Unpublished PhD, University of Toledo, Toledo, OH.

Mattingly, M. (2003). *A study of superintendents' practices of principal supervision and evaluation: A contrast of low performing and performing schools.* Unpublished EdD, University of Georgia, Athens, GA.

McEachern, R. (1990). *A study of stages of concern of a new intervention (computer-assisted instruction) in an elementary school.* Unpublished EdD, Florida State University, Tallahassee, FL.

McKenzie, W. (1996). *Investigative learning in undergraduate laboratory: An investigation into reform in science education.* Unpublished PhD, Virginia Polytechnic Institute and State University, Blacksburg, VA.

Menzel, N. (2001). *Manual handling workload and musculoskeletal discomfort in nursing personnel.* Unpublished PhD, University of South Florida, Tampa, FL.

Merriam, S. (1997). *Qualitative research and case study applications in education: Revised and expanded from case study research in education.* San Francisco, CA: Jossey-Bass.

Meyer, D. (2003). *Technology's relationship to issues connected to retention: A focus on rural mental health practitioners.* Unpublished PhD, Ohio University, Athens, OH.

Miles, M., & Huberman, A. M. (1994). *Qualitative data analysis* (2nd ed.). Thousand Oaks, CA: Sage.

Miller, C. (2004). *A case study of teacher hiring practices in award winning middle schools in Pennsylvania.* Unpublished EdD, University of Pittsburgh, Pittsburgh, PA.

Miller, L. (2003). *Qualitative investigation of intercollegiate coaches' perceptions of altruistic leadership.* Unpublished PhD, Ohio State University, Columbus, OH.

Morgan, S. (2004). *Advice to students: How to avoid plagiarism.* Retrieved on May 6, 2006, from http://www.services.unimelb .edu.au/plagiarism/advice.html#avoiding.

Mosser, J. W. (1993). *Predicting alumni/ae gift giving behavior: A structural equation model approach.* Unpublished PhD, University of Michigan, Ann Arbor, MI.

Murillo, J. E. (2005). *Murillo method: A guide.* Retrieved on May 7, 2005, from http://coe.csusb.edu/Murillo/method3.htm.

Murtagh, P., & Sterzl, K. (1995). *Guidelines for technical writing.* Retrieved on December 6, 2004, from http://www.itee.uq.edu .au/~elec3200/laboratory/repguide.ps.

National Health and Medical Research Council. (2000). *How to review the evidence: Systematic identification and review of the scientific literature.* Canberra, Australia: National Health and Medical Research Council.

Neill, S. (2003). *The identification of effective strategies for bond campaigns in Kansas school districts: An analysis of the beliefs of superintendents who conducted bond issue campaigns.* Unpublished EdD, Wichita State University, Wichita, KS.

Neuendorf, K. (2001). The content analysis guidebook online: Sage.

Nicolas, M. G. (2002). *A cross-cultural examination of individual values, worry, and mental health status.* Unpublished PhD, Pennsylvania State University, University Park, PA.

Nolan, K. (2004). *The influence of variations in shoe midsole density on the impact force and kinematics of landing in female volleyball players.* Unpublished PhD, University of Toledo, Toledo, OH.

Olson, J. (2004). *How do preservice teachers learn from early field experiences? Narratives from a cohort in an elementary teacher education program.* Unpublished PhD, University of Georgia, Athens, GA.

Ormondroyd, J., Engle, M., & Cosgrave, T. (2004). *Critically analyzing information sources.* Retrieved on April 7, 2005, from http://www.library.cornell.edu/olinuris/ref/research/skill26 .htm.

Pajares, F. (1997). *The elements of a proposal.* Retrieved on January 16, 2005, from http://www.emory.edu/EDUCATION/mfp/ proposal.html.

Paparone, C. (2003). *Applying the competing values framework to study organizational subcultures and system-wide planning efforts in a military university.* Unpublished PhD, Pennsylvania State University, University Park, PA.

Pariser. (1988). *The effects of telephone intervention on arthritis self-efficacy, depression, pain, and fatigue in older adults with arthritis.* Unpublished PhD, University of New Orleans, New Orleans, LA.

Partington, K. (2004). *The impact of self-esteem on academic achievement and aspirations of urban minority adolescents.* Unpublished PhD, Fairleigh Dickinson University, Madison, NJ.

Patton, M. (1990). *Qualitative evaluation and research methods* (2nd ed.). Newbury Park, CA: Sage.

Pfaffman, J. (2003). *Manipulating and measuring student engagement in computer-based instruction.* Unpublished PhD, Vanderbilt University, Nashville, TN.

Phillips, M. (2002). *The effectiveness of performance-based outcomes in a community college system.* Unpublished EdD, University of Florida, Tallahassee, FL.

Pidwirny, M. (2004). *Chapter 3: The science of physical geography—Hypothesis testing.* Retrieved on May 3, 2005, from http://www.physicalgeography.net/fundamentals/3f.html.

Poland, J. (2003). *Helpful tips for writing a thesis.* Retrieved on December 5, 2004, from http://www.hhs.csus.edu/CJ/Word_Docs/Graduate_Handbook_2003ed-Sept03-E-Helpful_Tips_for_Writing_a_Thesis.doc.

Porfeli, E. (2004). *A longitudinal study of a developmental-contextual model of work values during adolescence.* Unpublished PhD, Pennsylvania State University, University Park, PA.

Preiss, K. (2004). *The effects of exercise on college students' experience of anxiety.* Unpublished MA, Truman State University, Kirksville, MO.

Pringle, A. (1997). *A comparison of the cost analysis of three years of special education costs in Danville, Virginia.* Unpublished EdD, Virginia Polytechnic Institute and State University, Blacksburg, VA.

Purdue University. (2001). *Quoting, paraphrasing, and summarizing*. Online Writing Lab. Retrieved on April 24, 2005, from http://owl.english.purdue.edu/handouts/research/r_quotprsum .html.

Ragin, C., Nagel, J., & White, P. (2004). *Workshop on scientific foundations of qualitative research*. Washington, D.C.: National Science Foundation.

Rasmussen, C. (2004). *A community college's culture and its effect on student retention*. Unpublished EdD, Wichita State University, Wichita, KS.

Reed, G. (2004). *A forgiveness intervention with post-relationship psychologically abused women*. Unpublished PhD, University of Wisconsin–Madison, Madison, WI.

Ren, L. (2003). *Imagining China in the era of global consumerism and local consciousness: Media, mobility, and the Spring Festival*. Unpublished PhD, Ohio University, Athens, OH.

Reno, D. (2003). *Exploring the process of civic engagement: Phenomenological case study*. Unpublished EdD, North Carolina State University, Raleigh, NC.

Revere, D. (2004). *Avoiding plagiarism*. Retrieved on May 6, 2005, from http://courses.washington.edu/hsstudev/studev/ HowToAvoidPlagiarism.htm.

Ritter, J. M. (1999). *The development and validation of the self-efficacy beliefs about equitable science teaching and learning instrument for prospective elementary teachers*. Unpublished PhD, Pennsylvania State University, University Park, PA.

Romanello, M. (2001). *Cultural competence and reflective practice in physical therapy education*. Unpublished PhD, Miami University, Oxford, OH.

Salem, E. B. (2004). *Dissertation proposal writing tutorial: Conceptual framework*. Retrieved on January 19, 2005, from http://www.people.ku.edu/~ebben/tutorial_731.htm.

Shao, X. (2004). *Teacher training and curriculum reform in Chinese agricultural schools*. Unpublished PhD, Pennsylvania State University, University Park, PA.

Sheets, R. (1994). *The effects of training and experience on adult peer tutors in community colleges*. Unpublished EdD, Arizona State University, Phoenix, AZ.

Silverstein, G., & Sharp, L. (1997). Reporting the results of mixed method evaluations. In J. Frechtling & L. Sharp (Eds.), *User-friendly handbook for mixed method evaluations*. Washington, DC: National Science Foundation.

Skelton, J., & Edwards, S. (2000). The function of the discussion section in academic medical writing. *British Medical Journal, 320*, 1269–1270.

Smith, B. (1998). *Effects of home-school collaboration and different forms of parent involvement on reading achievement*. Unpublished EdD, Virginia Polytechnic and State University, Blacksburg, VA.

Smith, D. C. (2004). *Substance use attitudes and behaviors of students with learning disabilities*. Unpublished PhD, Ohio State University, Columbus, OH.

Strauss, A., & Corbin, J. (1990). *Basics of qualitative research: Grounded theory procedures and techniques*. Thousand Oaks, CA: Sage.

Suveg, C. (2003). *Emotion management in children with anxiety disorders: A focus on the role of emotion-related socialization processes*. Unpublished PhD, University of Maine, Orono, ME.

Sydenstricker-Neto, J. (1997). *Research design and mixed-method approach: A hands-on experience.* Retrieved on February 28, 2005, from http://www.socialresearchmethods.net/tutorial/Syden stricker/bolsa.html.

Talbot, A. (2004). *How much information do men really want? Information search behavior and decision rationale in a medical decision-making task for men.* Unpublished PhD, Pennsylvania State University, University Park, PA.

Taniguchi, S. (2004). *Outdoor education and meaningful learning: Finding the attributes of meaningful learning experiences in an outdoor education program.* Unpublished PhD, Brigham Young University, Salt Lake City, UT.

Taylor, D. (2001). *Writing a literature review in the health and social science work.* Retrieved on September 30, 2004, from http://www.utoronto.ca/hswriting/lit-review.htm.

Tellez, F. (2004). *Instrumental use of information in the design of the Chilean Secondary Education Reform.* Unpublished PhD, University of Pittsburgh, Pittsburgh, PA.

Thurman, S. (2004). *The glass ceiling as a mirror: How do women secondary school principals support school improvement?* Unpublished EdD, University of Cincinnati, Cincinnati, OH.

Trochim, W. (2001). *The research methods knowledge base* (2nd ed.). Cincinnati, OH: Atomic Dog Publishers.

Trochim, W. (2002a). *Research methods knowledge base.* Retrieved on October 29, 2004, from http://www .socialresearchmethods.net/kb.

Trochim, W. (2002b). *Research methods knowledge base: Analysis.* Retrieved on December 2, 2004, from http://www .socialresearchmethods.net/kb/analysis.htm.

Tufte, E. (1997). *Visual explanation: Images and quantities, evidence and narrative*. Cheshire, CT: Graphic Press.

University of California. (2001). *Dissertation proposal workshop*. Institute of International Studies, Berkeley. Retrieved on August 23, 2004, from http://globetrotter.berkeley.edu/DissPropWorkshop/nuts&bolts/question.html.

University of Chicago Press. (2003). *The Chicago manual of style* (15th ed.). Chicago: University of Chicago Press.

University of San Francisco. (2004). *Format for research proposal*. College of Professional Studies. Retrieved on January 20, 2005, from http://www.cps.usfca.edu/ob/resources/format.htm.

University of South Dakota. (2005). *12 components: Evaluating qualitative design*. Retrieved on May 10, 2005, from http://www.usd.edu/ahed/analysis.cfm.

University of the Witwatersrand. (2005). *Preparing your research proposal*. Retrieved on May 12, 2005, from http://www.wits.ac.za/education/phdproposal.html.

University of Wisconsin–Madison. (2004). *Review of literature*. UW-Madison Writing Center. Retrieved on September 10, 2004, from http://www.wisc.edu/writing/Handbook/ReviewofLiterature.html.

van Teijlingen, E., & Hundley, E. (2001). The importance of pilot studies. *Social Research UpDate* (Winter).

Wabuyele, L. (2003). *Understanding teachers' and administrators' perceptions and experiences towards computer use in Kenyan classrooms: A case study of two schools.* Unpublished PhD, Ohio University, Athens, OH.

Waddell, C. (2004). *The effects of negotiated written feedback within formative assessment on fourth grade students' motivation and goal orientations.* Unpublished PhD, University of Missouri–St. Louis, St. Louis, MO.

Walonick, D. (2005). *Elements of a research proposal and report.* Retrieved on October 26, 2005, from http://www.statpac.com/research-papers/research-proposal.htm.

Watson, G. (1997). *Beyond the psychological contract: Ideology and the economic social contract in a restructuring environment.* Unpublished PhD, Virginia Polytechnic Institute and State University, Blacksburg, VA.

Williams, S. (2004). *A meta-analysis of the effectiveness of distance education in allied health science programs.* Unpublished PhD, University of Cincinnati, Cincinnati, OH.

Wong, P. (2002). *How to write a research proposal.* Retrieved on February 9, 2005, from http://www.meaning.ca/articles/print/writing_research_proposal_may02.htm.

World Health Organization. (2004). *Guidelines for writing a research proposal (protocol).* Regional Office for Southeast Asia, Communicable Diseases Department. Retrieved on February 9, 2005, from http://w3.whosea.org/en/Section10/Section1843_8150.htm.

Yin, R. (2003). *Case study research: Design and methods* (3rd ed., vol. 5). Thousand Oaks, CA: Sage.

About the Author

Raymond Calabrese, professor in the College of Education at Wichita State University, serves on the graduate faculty in the Department of Educational Leadership. He received his Ed.D. from the University of Massachusetts at Amherst in education. He has experience as a public school teacher, counselor, and principal. In academe, Dr. Calabrese has published a number of academic books, including *Leadership through Excellence*, *The Leadership Assignment: Creating Change*, and *Leadership for Safe Schools*. Moreover, he has an extensive research agenda focusing on alienation, social justice, appreciative inquiry, and urban education. His published research has been recognized internationally. The College of Education at Wichita State University recognized him as "researcher of the year" for the academic year 2004–2005.

Dr. Calabrese's work in urban and rural schools includes involving doctoral students on action research teams. He guides them to focus on the assets of students, teachers, administrators, and the community in the urban environment. His doctoral students consistently present research at the prestigious Annual Meeting of the American Educational Research Association, publish field research in refereed journals, and collaborate with urban and rural school administrators and teachers to transform their schools. Dr. Calabrese was motivated to write this book because of his work with these students and witnessing the challenges they faced in writing their dissertations.